Strategic Realization of Millennium Development Goals

Emmanuel Edeh, a ROLE MODEL

Ezechi Chukwu PhD

authorHOUSE®

AuthorHouse™
1663 Liberty Drive
Bloomington, IN 47403
www.authorhouse.com
Phone: 1-800-839-8640

Published by AuthorHouse 11/26/2013

ISBN: 978-1-4918-2319-4 (sc)
ISBN: 978-1-4918-2318-7 (hc)
ISBN: 978-1-4918-2317-0 (e)

Library of Congress Control Number: 2013917693

Table of Contents

Part One
Edeh's Formative Background

Part Two
Edeh's Social Philosophy

Introduction

The question of how to improve humans' standard of living has been a dominant issue throughout the history of human society, from the ancient civilizations of Mesopotamia, Egypt, and Greece to our societies today, and throughout the various forms of societal organization: republic, *polis, civitas,* and state. Governments and international organizations today continue to champion policies that seek to improve human welfare, and the media are pervaded with stories of both national and international efforts and various institutional measures to better our lot.

In the international arena, the League of Nations was formed after World War I, which lasted from 1914 to 1918 and was horrific because of the human slaughter that took place. Thereafter, world powers believed that the only way they could avoid a repetition of such a disaster was to create an international body to maintain world peace by sorting out international disputes. The member countries chose to base the organization in Geneva, Switzerland, because this country did not fight in World War I and the Red Cross, another international organization, was already based in Switzerland.

Unfortunately, the League of Nations could not prevent future wars, and after World War II, it was replaced by the United Nations (UN).This new international organization was founded on October 24, 1945, by fifty-one countries committed to maintaining international peace and security and to develop friendly relations among nations. These member organizations also sought to improve the lives of people by conquering hunger, disease, and illiteracy; encouraging respect for all people's rights and freedom; and harmonizing the actions of nations to achieve these goals.

'UN at a Glance', says that the UN has 193 member states and more than 100,000 peacekeepers engaged in 16 peace operations. According to this UN's website, "As a result of its unique international character and the powers vested in its founding Charter, the Organization can take action on a wide range of issues, and provide a forum for its 193 Member States to express their views, through the General Assembly, the Security Council, the Economic and Social Council and other bodies and committees." The work of the United Nations in peacekeeping, peacebuilding, conflict prevention, and provision of humanitarian assistance extends to every corner of the globe.

The United Nations and its specialized agencies, funds, and programs affect our lives and make the world a better place in many other ways as well. In general, it works on a broad range of issues including sustainable development, the environment, refugee protection, disaster relief, counterterrorism, disarmament, nonproliferation, and more in order to achieve its goals and coordinate efforts for a safer world (UN 2012).

Most of the objectives of the United Nations are lofty and abstract. Therefore, to achieve them, the UN has adopted Millennium Development Goals (MDGs), eight goals for international development that were officially established following the Millennium Summit of the United Nations in 2000, as a result of the adoption of the United Nations Millennium Declaration. The goals are:

- Eradication of extreme poverty and hunger
- Achievement of universal primary education
- Promotion of gender equality and empowerment of women
- Reduction of child mortality rates
- Improvement of maternal health
- Combating HIV/AIDS, malaria, and other diseases
- Ensuring environmental sustainability
- Development of a global partnership for development

All 193 member states and at least 23 other international organizations have agreed to achieve these goals by the year 2015. Since the adoption of the MDGs, progress towards reaching them has been uneven. Some countries have achieved many of the goals, whereas others are not on track to realizing them. Each of the goals includes specific targets along the way and dates for achieving those targets.

As a kind of incentive to various countries of the world, especially the heavily indebted countries, to enhance the realization of the Millennium Development Goals, many international banking organizations forgave debts to allow these developing countries to channel resources to the

MDGs, especially in the areas of poverty alleviation, health and education. A UN conference in September 2010 reviewed progress and adopted a global action plan to achieve the antipoverty goals by their 2015 target date and also made new commitments to women's and children's health and formed new initiatives in the worldwide battle against hunger and diseases.

Knowledge of peace efforts from the League of Nations and the United Nations compels one to ask several important questions: Has the world achieved global peace? Can we say that the UN Charter has been successfully executed so far? Have governments around the world effectively made steps to ending the hazards of hunger, environmental degradation, poor education, health-related disasters, ethnic, regional, religious, national, and international wars?

The Millennium Development Goals seem to have finally given the world reason to say yes to those questions. The importance given to the MDGs by the collaboration of the UN with financial institutions and donor agencies made many in the world believe that the MDGs would usher in a golden era in the twenty-first century. Unfortunately, a comprehensive meet up with the 2015 deadline for achieving the MDGs remains a fantasy and the goals in some areas seem more academic than practical; even with changing government policies all over the globe, the United Nations' apparent commitment, and the media hype surrounding the MDGs.

One cannot sincerely doubt the United Nations' good intentions in introducing the MDGs as a reasonable solution to human and environmental ailments across the globe, but it is one thing to generate a good idea or policy and quite another to set out realistic steps to actually achieve it. Since various efforts of the UN, in collaboration with governments around the world in line with the MDGs are yet to fully achieve the desired goals, it is then necessary that these institutions turn to functional and tested methods such as that of Fr. Prof. Emmanuel Edeh. The targeted impact Edeh has made on humanity and the method through which he has attained them, are indubitably worth considering.

As the title of this work depicts, the underscore is to proffer strategies through which Millennium Development Goals could be realized from the perspective of Edeh's philosophy and work. Just as the history of politics in South Africa is incomplete without apartheid, so is the discussion of the Millennium Development Goals, incomplete without Edeh's unparalleled contributions. Edeh's invaluable individual import in the eight targeted areas of MDGs is amazing and justifiably paints his methods as a prototype in the concrete realization of MDGs.

To discuss Emmanuel Edeh's perspective, this work makes a critical inquiry into Edeh's philosophy and identifies how it has shaped his prodigious contributions to humanity in line with the MDGs. This work then discusses how we can consider Edeh's work as an effective archetype for the strategic realization of the Millennium Development Goals.

The book is divided into two major parts. Part 1 looks at Edeh's background, including his mother's influence and his religious formation. It also investigates his concept of *mma-di*, which translates to "good that is." With the understanding of the concept of *mma-di* as the key to Edeh's philosophy of being, part 2 then delves into his social philosophy, Edeh's Philosophy of Thought and Action (EPTAism), his concept of practical and effective charity and Edeh's Charity Peace Model (ECPM).

The work then critically assesses how Edeh's notions of community and *omenani*, or tradition, formed the precursors to his contributions in line with the MDGs. Subsequently, it takes a general look at the Millennium Development Goals and assesses the progress made so far, as noted in the UN's *Millennium Development Goals Report 2012*. It further investigates the current challenges organizations and nations face in a bid to achieve the goals and makes recommendations in tune with EPTAism.

In this section, it needs to be noted that the work treats MDGs Number 4: Reduction of Child Mortality, MDGs Number 5: Improvement of Maternal Health and MDGs Number 6: Combating HIV/AIDS, Malaria, and Other Diseases in one section entitled: "Edeh: A Model of Sustainable Health-Care Delivery." Finally, the work summarizes the major argument and makes further recommendations.

Part One

Edeh's Formative Background

1.1: Family Background: Mother's Influence

Growth is a gradual process and no success story is complete without the consideration of external influence. Humans create society but society invariably shapes humans. The nucleus of society and the foundation of human growth is the family. It is in the family where a person spends his or her formative years and it is very difficult to talk of the exact point where that person's maturity begins; for the point where one stage of development ends, the next begins since human development exists on a continuum. A person is shaped by the biological, social, and environmental factors that he is exposed to throughout life.

The family provides the foundation for growth and a person's most basic education. Parents, especially mothers, are the window through which infants first perceive and access the world, providing infants their first glimpse of society. The role of the family in determining the future and life of the child is inarguable. Family influence is instrumental in determining the career or vocation children take on later in life, which in turn defines who they are socially.

Humans are ontologically equal but socially unequal. Social inequality is determined by so many factors and one cannot rule out the fact that the type of education and orientation a child is nurtured with often have logical correlation with the success or otherwise of that child during adulthood. Some people are privileged in the society today as leaders and source of inspiration to the world because of the seed of service and humility already sown in them during infancy. This is typical of the formation the young Emmanuel Edeh received from his family, especially his mother at the early years of his life.

Emmanuel Mathew Paul Edeh was born into a typical traditional African family: his father was the head of the family, and his mother was the helper of her husband as she also took care of the children and managed the domestic affairs of the family. It is noteworthy that "In African traditional communities women hold an indispensable position" (Kayode 1984, 6).

Not only that they help their husbands in farm work, family businesses and the general upkeep of their homes, they are also in charge of the domestic activities of their families and by that act closer to their children.

In this vein, African women equally contribute like men in the building of the community and the actualization of various human potentials, just as Buscaglia notes: "The world, too, is mostly unactualized potential, waiting upon us for its realization" (1978, 19). Edeh's mother, Madam Elizabeth Edeh Ani Onovo, had enormous influence in shaping the Emmanuel Edeh the world knows today. She inspired him to actualize his potentials.

In *Mothers & Sons: Raising Boys to Be Men*, Vredevelt emphasizes the role mothers play in supporting their successful male children, and she states: "The more I research, the more I find prominent men applauding their mothers for planting seeds of success during their childhood … They selflessly sacrificed personal comfort and dedicated themselves to helping their little boys become men of dignity and strength" (1988, 15). This is an accurate picture of the role Edeh's mother played for the young Emmanuel.

Edeh's mother, popularly called Mama Omeogo (Mother of Charity) was a woman of courage, faith, and vigor who instilled the virtues of charity and love in her son. While recounting the life and works of Edeh, his friend, Remy Onyewuenyi (2010) describes Mama Omeogo as a generous woman who loved and cared for all the children in the neighborhood. She would buy food and wears for the neighborhood children and distributed them as gifts when she returned home. Out of the goodness of her heart, she would help other mothers to bathe and prepare their children for the day, and in some occasions, she would even cook food to share with the children.

Being a parent is a worthy task, but how we exercise the parenthood is more important. When we care for other people's children, we develop society and build bridges between the shores of humanity. Recalling Edeh's mother as a caring and loving mother, Onyewuenyi continues: "Her meticulous, unreserved and continuous practice of charity towards the little children and her neighbours merited for her the nicknames 'Mama Omeogo', 'Mama Umuaka Nine' and 'Mama Anyi'[Mother of Charity, Mother of All Little Children, and Our Mother]" (Onyewuenyi 2010, 3). She exercised motherhood for the children around her without discrimination.

The care and love Edeh's mother gave to those beyond her immediate family affected the little Emmanuel Edeh's belief system, emotions and circumstances. When we care, we do something that makes other people feel better about life. When we care, our concern improves other individuals' situations. To care therefore is both an assignment of value to another and a function of the heart.

Certainly, not all great mothers raise great children. Nevertheless, mothers can develop the skills and virtues inherent in children in their care. The young Emmanuel's mother also gave him warmth, love, and comfort, providing for his emotional needs, engendering a sense of security in him and inspired him with her charity. Bernie Siegel seems to see nurturing of children in the same way Edeh's mother did:

> When we raise a generation of children with compassion, when parents make sure that their children know that they are loved, when teachers truly educate and not just inform, and when the clergy of every faith reminds us that we are all children of God, we will have a planet inhabited by the human family, where our differences are used for recognition and not persecution, where we recognize that we are all the same color inside (2004, 41).

Naturally, parents generally desire that their children be fair, honest, reliable, loving and lovable, kind, and compassionate and also that they be law abiding citizens, ambitious, and hardworking. These are wonderful ideals which are easily imbibed by children when their parents not only profess them but model them. According to Vredevelt (1997), he who wants his son to become a man and bring peace and happiness to others should give him opportunities to do it while the child is growing up. She insists: "Be an example. Morals are better caught than taught. The best way to pass on values to your children is through living them" (204). This was how Madam Elizabeth went about parenting and how her son Emmanuel learned these values.

Emmanuel Edeh grew up seeing and feeling the charity, love, and care his mother gave others, as a result, Mama Omeogo instilled in him the knowledge that there is joy and love in giving and sharing; by so doing, charity became a foundation for his life. In Mama Omeogo, little Emmanuel had not only a mother and a loved one but also a role model, adviser, and hallmark of love, selflessness, empathy and service to the community. In his mother, the young Emmanuel found a safe space because "The overriding concern is that children should at all times be in safe, supervised, controlled spaces. Outside these spaces their safety, and with it their very experience of childhood, is deemed to be at risk" (Nieuwenhuys 2003, 99).

The safe space, accompanied with good upbringing provided fertile ground for the development of Edeh's crusade of peace in his adulthood. Kutai (1999) emphasizes that youths are leaders of tomorrow and our understanding of their welfare today determines our society's security of tomorrow. The care of Edeh's mother for the children in her neighborhood demonstrated her belief in this idea.

The important lesson here is that our character is molded by the training we receive from our families and the behaviour we see them demonstrate when we are at the formative stage of our lives. We learn from and depend on those who nurse and nurture us. From them, we derive the tastes and even prejudices that cleave to us nearly all the years of our lives. We easily understand our mothers' verbal and nonverbal languages and learn to speak them, inadvertently embracing their mannerisms and ways. In adulthood, we recall how much we owe to our parents for sowing unquantifiable seeds of value in us in our infancy.

The fireside where Mama Omeogo cooked the food she distributed to the neighborhood kids acted as a school where Emmanuel Edeh learned the values that would lead him to become a clergy, professor, thinker, role model, motivator, servant leader, peace breeder, peacebuilder and peacemaker. For children, imitation is a much stronger method of learning than memorization. When children are allowed to practice what they are taught, those lessons have a much stronger effect on their minds than those they are taught by lectures only. In this way, Edeh's mother was a unique community builder, as Abanuka explains: "Through his relationships and actions in the community, the individual comes to understand the meaning of the community and can contribute to the community's self-understanding" (1994, 28).

For the young Emmanuel, Mama Omeogo was also a living example of reverence in prayer to grace and the word of God, of verbal expression, temper, diligence, temperance, faith and humility. Emmanuel copied and practiced what he saw Mama Elizabeth, his model doing. Not only did Emmanuel understand his mother's reasoning and lecturing, her wise commands and good advice, he also understood his mother's life, which was worthy of emulation.

Generally, a parent who tries to train a child without also setting a good example is building with one hand and pulling down with the other. Children hardly learn habits that their parents' actions show that they despise and do not walk down paths that their parents do not walk on. Mama Omeogo knew that to teach a child what one does not practice is to embark on a journey without a destination.

Home is the place where children usually form their habits and where the foundations of their character are laid and mothers, being the closest people to their children in the early stages of their lives, instill those habits that can make or mar the future of their children, consciously or unconsciously. In fact, a parent's word should reconcile with his or her action for it to bear the desired fruit before the child.

The practical charity and love Edeh's mother demonstrated were worth more to Emmanuel compared with the reading of volumes of literature on peace and charity in his adulthood. While looking back on his childhood, Edeh would likely express similar feeling to those Jonathon Lazear expresses when recounting a dream in *Remembrance of Mother*: "It is only then that I realize that I'm beginning to feel my mother's loss. My dream has been a very memorable conversation with her; we are laughing, reminiscing, hugging, and commiserating. It is a perfect dream of a person who is gone. We are totally in sync and happy. Oh, how I miss her" (1994, 69).

When Edeh today advocates practical and effective charity, one can see that he professes what is an intrinsic part of his being, for he saw his mother demonstrate charity in practical and concrete terms and he has seen and experienced the power of peace. He witnessed throughout his mother's life the unity, compassion, and communion that charity could instill in a community. The seed Mama Omeogo planted in Edeh is described well in the words of Ross: "Our lives manifest our dominant thoughts. Just as whatever we plant grows, that which we focus our attention on multiplies. Whatever we put into our minds comes out in our lives" (1983, 49).

1.2: Religious Formation

In *The Adventurers: Ordinary People with Special Callings*, Diana Forrest takes a look at the mind-set of some exemplary Christians, including St. Francis of Assisi, Mother Teresa of Calcutta and Fr. Damien of Molokai, affirming that "they all have in common the fact that they were willing to risk their careers, their friendships and family ties, and even their lives because they believed there was something God wanted them to do. They all proved dramatically that being a Christian is an adventure" (1955, 7). To term a Christian life "an adventure," Forrest implies that Christianity goes beyond make-believe and rhetoric, that it is a quest with accompanying duties and challenges. Emmanuel Edeh seems to have understood Christianity in this way, too, when he opted to become a Roman Catholic priest.

Like the other adventurers Forrest mentions, Fr. Edeh did not allow anything or anyone to stand between him and his God in the accomplishment of his assignment. In fact, Forrest clarifies that all the adventurers in her book experienced trials and even personal tragedy in living out their callings. St. Francis of Assisi, for instance, witnessed some of his original ideas being distorted even though his movement was in crescendo. Mother Teresa was so shy that she could not cope with the huge crowds with cameras that continued to besiege her. Like them, Edeh the focused adventurer persevered in his quest and accomplished his own mission, too, despite distractions and difficulties.

Unfortunately, many people did not understand that when Fr. Edeh disallowed cameras to record services in his ministry, he did so because he believed that popularity and praise belonged strictly to God and that publicity for himself, a mere instrument and steward in the service of Chineke (God who Creates),was uncalled for. He was rather focused and tenaciously committed to those values which pleased *Chineke* rather than appealing to the figment of people's fantasy. Those who did not identify with him then, today, obviously bear with him. He knew his mission and basically avoided unnecessary distractions.

In "Africa and the Challenge of Integral (Integrated) Formation of Priests in (the Understanding of) the 21st Century Synod of Africa," Otonko (2009) emphasizes the fact that priests are the subjects of high expectations, as a result, priestly formation is a demanding challenge. Creating a dichotomy among African priests by comparing them to two large ships, Otonko states: "In one ship are the many priests who are living out true and authentic lives of witness, with total commitment to their vocation; performing their priestly functions with faithfulness and diligence; living lives of constant fidelity to their religious vows; and paying adequate attention to their cultic and pastoral duties" (157). Like this category of priests, Edeh embarked on his pastoral duties with a great sense of the need to care and serve without necessarily being served.

With the knowledge of the spirit of love and charity that permeated the young Emmanuel Edeh's psyche, one may not be surprised that he felt called to religious life and it was no accident that he pitched his tent in a religious vocation in order to perpetuate charity and peace in which he was immersed as a child. Onyewuenyi (2010) recalls that Emmanuel was a bright pupil who completed his primary education with flying colors in 1962 before he enrolled in the Holy Ghost Juniorate Ihiala for his secondary education the following year.

The Holy Ghost Juniorate was founded in 1953 by the Irish Holy Ghost Missionaries as a seminary and secondary school for the cultivation of young boys who had the intention of becoming priests and missionaries. Throughout his tenure at the school, he was very active in school affairs and was above all a very disciplined and rule-abiding student.

> During his Junior Seminary days, he was very influenced by Rev. Fr. Patrick Animba, a native of Nomey and the first indigenous priest of Nkanu land, who was very instrumental in the nursing of his religious vocation and care for the poor. From Rev. Fr. Animba, he learnt to hand over his entire life to the practice of charity (Onyewuenyi 2010, 10).

Edeh remained dedicated to these principles even while studying at the Holy Ghost Scholasticate in Awo-Omama, where he completed his philosophical studies in 1970. During the Nigerian Civil War of 1967–1970,

7

the novitiate and Spiritan formation houses situated in Awo-Omama, in present-day Orlu Senatorial Zone of Imo State, were shut down because the expatriate Irish missionaries who ran them refused to leave Biafra on the order of the federal government of Nigeria and the Holy Ghost seminarians resident in those houses continued their education at Bigard Memorial Seminary Enugu.

Emmanuel Edeh was one of the victims of this institutional setback, but that did not deter him from his commitment to realize his vocation. The painful experiences of that period only fortified his zeal. In this way, Edeh seems to agree with Nouwen, who states in *With Burning Hearts* that "Indeed, the conflicts in our personal lives as well as the conflicts on regional, national, or world scales are *our* conflicts and only by claiming responsibility for them can we move beyond them—choosing a life of forgiveness, peace, and love"(1994, 32). If Edeh had not been a child of destiny and one with firm knowledge of his mission and a firm commitment to actualizing it, he may have given up his mission during this thorny time.

Edeh's religious education continued to shape the spirit of care and simplicity that were already in him and offered him a better opportunity to practice what he knew best—charity. His religious formation made him stronger. As Nouwen explains, "The great temptation of our lives is to deny our role as chosen people and so allow ourselves to be trapped in the worries of our daily lives" (1994, 49). Edeh did not of course fall into this temptation and allow the worries of the closure of his seminary during the Nigeria Civil War or the wrath of the war itself to distract him.

In fact, he saw the war as an opportunity to indulge in practical humanitarian work, as Onyewuenyi says: "The civil war experience was a form of training for him in the care of the needy and suffering. As a seminarian he participated in the works of Caritas International—an International Catholic Non-Governmental Organization that played a major role in providing food, clothing and medicine for Biafran children, refugees and displaced persons" (2010, 13). Dedication and focus are important in the life of anyone who desires to succeed and Edeh seems to have understood this in his days as a seminarian and learned that, as Nouwen remarks, "every time there is a real encounter leading from despair to hope and from bitterness to gratitude, we will see some of the darkness being dispelled and life, once again, breaking through the boundaries of death" (1994, 90–91).

The seminary in Awo-Omama offered him the opportunity to participate actively in the humanitarian work of Caritas International. During this period, he worked in the various centers that distributed relief materials around the Holy Ghost novitiate. Onyewuenyi (2010) notes that Edeh not only served the Biafran children food and gave them clothes, he also found time to play with them and to teach them songs and prayers.

Afterwards, from the time he joined Bigard Memorial Seminary in Enugu for his theological studies, to the time he was ordained a Catholic priest of the Holy Ghost Congregation on April 19, 1976, it was evident that the future priest was fully prepared for the work of charity and peace he was destined for. The young Fr. Emmanuel Edeh must have conceived his vocation in line with "The Divine Maternity and the Priesthood" from *The Fair Flower of Eden* by Rev. Forrest when he states:

> The priesthood is a dignity of indescribable grandeur, which raises its recipient to a dazzling height, beyond the reach of natural vision. It is a dignity which stamps the soul of the aspirant with an ineffaceable character, whereby he is endowed with a godlike of offering sacrifice, and producing grace in the souls upon which he exercises his sacramental influence ... [T]he priest offers unto the Sovereign Majesty the august sacrifice, wherein the Spotless Lamb of God is truly immolated, and he is also appointed by the Church to exercise a mediation of prayer between the human race and its Creator (1946, 69).

This "sacramental influence" was a major factor in shaping Edeh's mission of love, peace and charity to maturity. No doubt, the grace in Edeh's ministry, the Pilgrimage Center of Eucharistic Adoration and Special Marian Devotion, which started like a mustard seed in 1985, is reflective of the continuous "mediation of prayer between the human race and its Creator," as Rev. Forrest puts it. The priesthood afforded Edeh the opportunity to dedicate uninterrupted time and boundless energy to the inspiration of the gospel and service to his fellow humans. His religious education brought him closer to God.

During his subsequent studies in the United States, Edeh continued to practice charity and when he returned to Nigeria, his provincial superior, Very Rev. Fr. James Okoye, noticed Fr. Edeh's special flair for caring and decided to post him to a parish instead of assigning him a teaching position in the seminary as was originally planned. Since then, Edeh has continued to build upon the foundation laid by his mother, which was reinforced secondly by his Christian religious background; thirdly, by the practicality of African philosophy, coupled with the practical and effective charity of his mission of peace.

1.3: The Origin of Edeh's Philosophy of Mma-di

Evidence abounds that human action is informed by reason. When a man eats, he does that because he wants to satisfy his appetite for food. When he studies, he does that because he wants to learn in order to be informed. He is religious because he wants to maintain his spiritual well-being, and he is ambitious because he wants to better his standard of living. However, people sometimes do the same thing for different reasons and sometimes these reasons conflict. When such a situation arises, we will struggle to find the reason that best justifies our action.

In the process of evaluating what we ought to do in any circumstance, thereby minimizing the element of luck, we embark on both rational deliberation and moral reasoning. The need to choose the proper rational justification and moral justification is very important, since right or wrong, the action will have consequences. Further, the rightness or wrongness of an action should equally be determined, putting into consideration the effects they have on us.

Humans are moral beings who constantly evaluate their circumstances and actions and consequently make decisions accordingly. We use reasoning to make choices for almost everything imaginable, starting with our basic needs for shelter, food, clothing and family and extending to all areas of human endeavor, including art, music, literature, religion, and culture—the output of our intellectual prowess and imaginative creativity. Unlike other animals, which respond only to their immediate sensory perceptions to meet purely material needs, humans, as privileged beings, pursue both material and intangible, spiritual goals, inventing and interpreting signs and symbols along the way. We appreciate the order and harmony in the universe and appropriate meaning to life in our continuous quest for happiness. Humans in fact possess dignity and worth as carriers of body and soul, of material and spiritual entities.

Edeh sees in humans not only the material and the spiritual but also another fundamental nature: *mma-di* ("good that is"), informed by his articulation of African philosophy through Igbo metaphysics. Edeh remarks that "Igbo man derives a notion of being from his concept of himself" (1985, 97). He goes on to emphasize that when an Igbo man is confronted with the question of how he becomes aware of what is, he responds that it begins with an awareness of who he is as a visible and concrete instance of what is.

A review of the answers to a questionnaire in *Towards an Igbo Metaphysics* used during the course of his investigation Edeh (1985) reveals that the question, "How do you know that things are?" was answered with, "I know this at least from the fact that human beings are, that we are" (98). Once more, we see that the notion of being is derived from the concept of our being. We can then draw an inference from this concept to the unity of all beings as thus: existence is the common denominator of all beings.

It is vital to our discussion that we understand the Igbo milieu, which is Edeh's investigative terrain, in harmony with the principle of contextual theory of action, which states that action has "implicit reference to some set of rules, norms, practices, principles, or standards in terms of which the action is described and can be evaluated" (Shaffer 1968, 94). Therefore, a good understanding of the Igbo social environment is necessary, as the environment comprises all things that affect the existence and development of the individual and the society.

Philosophically, although the environment is a concept of varied components, it is still a complex system of interactions, with a person at the center of the system and its management. In this vein, Edeh's experience of the Igbo-African environment is interconnected with his philosophy. Since a man and his environment are inseparable, this interplay between man and environment naturally creates equity between the two, leading man to influence the environment and the environment to shape man.

Acknowledging this complementary influence, Edeh (1985) states that the Igbo word for man is *madu*. He goes on to trace the etymology of *madu*, noting that it is a short form of *mma-di*, with *mma* being the Igbo word for "good" or "the good" and *di* deriving from *idi*, the Igbo verb "to be." We see this verb used in *okwute-di* ("stone that is") and *osisi-di* ("tree that is"). This leads Edeh to the conclusion that the combination of *mma* and *di—mma-di*—means "good that is."

So far, we have seen Edeh's reasoning in the context of Igbo thought pattern through which he arrived at the notion of man as *mma-di*. According to Raz (1975), we use reason to explain, guide, evaluate and make assertions about people's behaviour and ways of life. It is with this knowledge that we can also know what we ought to do, and this is where Edeh's concept of *mma-di* provides us with a logical link between our being and all beings.

To this effect, Edeh (1985) categorically states that the Igbo notion of *mma-di* must be comprehended in the context of creation because the notion of good for the Igbos is derived from divine creation. Hence, to say that man is good that is does not mean that man is "good in se", for no one else could be said to be "good in se" except God. Then what is the true nature of the good of man? Edeh specifies that the good of man which only participates in the goodness of God is "good per se".

Edeh substantiates the argument of the supreme goodness of God with unique Igbo expressions exclusively appropriated to God, such as, *So Chukwu di mma ezie* (Only God is good in the real sense), and *Onye di mma belu so Chukwu?* (Who is good but God?). Thus: "The Igbos share the religious idea common to many peoples that man's goodness is participated. Man is 'good that is' in the sense that, having been created by God, he is a product of his maker and hence shares in the being of his maker, the highest good" (Edeh 1985, 100–101). In a similar vein, Igbo names like *Chi-amaka* and *Chi-bu-mma* mean that "God is the good."

Metaphysically speaking, the existence of a being is derived from its maker. When we say that something is "good that is," we indirectly affirm the entity that makes such a being. Edeh therefore concludes that "this application is possible on the basis that all things are created by God and hence the notion of 'good that is' can be attributed to them" (1985, 102). The participatory nature of *mma-di*, of our deriving goodness from the divine, is the point at which we can say that *mma-di* is universal.

1.4: The Sacredness of Mma-di

The renowned French thinker Jacques Maritain (2005) observes that the first thing that practical philosophy must tackle is the question of what the ultimate end or absolute good of humans is. What Maritain means here is that practical philosophy must study the actions by which we approach or deviate from achieving our ultimate goal. This could be done he argues by examining our inner machinery and dynamics and what constitutes our moral character—that is, what qualifies us to be morally good or bad. The central argument here is that ethics must study the ultimate reason for every action. Hence, putting into consideration both the proximate and ulterior principles from which those acts emanate, in order to know their moral virtues or otherwise.

The inner machinery and the factors that constitute our moral character as Maritain mentions do have a link with each other. In the Igbo worldview, man is considered a moral being, since he is naturally good, considering also the source of his being which is "good in se" (God). Hence: "the Igbo ontological position that all things are good because of creation presupposes two things: first, that God is the absolute good who causes the good in all beings; second, that God's very act of creating is synonymous with his act of causing good in what he creates" (Edeh 1985, 102). This makes it clearer why Edeh is committed to the good of people.

Edeh articulates an African philosophy that is more practical than speculative. He describes it in his later work as thus:

> The distinctive feature of African philosophy is that it cannot be thought of in terms of an objective, abstract science as was fashionable in Western Philosophy. In African Philosophy we are dealing with a practical theoretical science in the sense that by nature African Metaphysics is a lived philosophy rather than a purely theoretical or scientific enterprise. To capture and present what is truly an

African way of viewing life and existence, beings and Being,
one has to come to grips with the interplay of thought and
action (Edeh 2006, 3).

Edeh makes us understand that in Igbo metaphysics, we see the African
mind as a holistic and clear picture of man: "This philosophy offers people
an ideal of human dignity based upon the belief that all beings created by
God are ontologically good and deserving of care and respect" (Edeh 2006,
4). He continues, "Igbo Metaphysics is saying that we should accept man as
good within the context of creation; a confirmation of the mystery of man's
dealing with God … I am saying that this affirmation must be concretized
in practical terms. If you accept man as 'good that is' we must go ahead and
do our best and establish realities that depict man as such" (2006, 5). The
point here is that man should be treated as purely good that is and it should
be acknowledged that he deserves nothing to the contrary. Therefore, the
sacredness of *mma-di* is understood best within the context of the big picture
of human life, which is derived from the divine source.

The divine origin of man in the Igbo thought pattern is an indication
that the Igbos see life beyond the here and now. They comprehend humans
as an extension of their maker, as having an extraterrestrial bond. Edeh
states, "The Igbos have a very high regard for life. Life is not a personal
business which can be tampered with at will. Life and existence are not
properties that belong wholly and entirely to individuals. They belong also
to the community of being formed by dead ancestors, the living and over
and above all, they belong to Chineke, the author and sustainer of life and
existence" (Edeh 1985, 57). As Edeh sees it, our life must be viewed in this
big-picture context.

Ellin also explains the concept of the big picture as: "one way in which
life is said to attain meaning is by being part of some larger scheme of things.
We call this 'big picture' meaning. Those who think that life has no meaning
think that there is no big picture of which our lives are a part" (Ellin 1995,
318). Ellin here seems to reinforce a similar belief held by the Igbos who
by linking their origin to God, the source of all existing beings, link the
ultimate justification for their lives with God as well. Ellin also remarks:
"Each person's actions make sense only in the context of the large scheme of
things" (1995, 319). One who does not see the big picture may treat *mma-di*

with disdain, thereby undermining the sacredness of human nature and calling.

After articulating the African thought pattern through the Igbo metaphysics in 1985, Edeh took it a step further and became deeply involved with implementing this philosophy in existential realities. Through this interaction between thought and action, he manifested that African philosophy is genuine since it leads to authentic human development, as Okwudili informs us:

> It is evident that thought cannot stand by itself and have merit. It needs to be marched with action so that the thought process itself becomes fulfilling to the individual and enriching to the society. Any direction philosophy may take to improve on thought will have to start with an awareness of the inherent values of the action. (Okwudili, 201: 156).

For *mma-di* to live a fulfilled life, the sacredness of that life should be evident. However, it is not enough to proclaim it, for it requires a complement of concrete existential practices to be valid. Egbekpalu (2011) observes from an in-depth look into Edeh's philosophical anthropology that it is a well-articulated and deeply analyzed ontology of man because Edeh's focus on the connection between the being of man and his ultimate purpose of existence, or destiny, equips us with a sound understanding of man from his genuine metaphysical-anthropological dimension.

Part Two

Edeh's Social Philosophy

Part 1 of the work has given us a general idea of Edeh's background, beginning with his mother's influence on him in his early life. His mother, a peace lover and helper to the community, imparted a devotion to charity to young Emmanuel and this informed Edeh's choice to pursue a priestly vocation. This foundation then led to his intellectual inquiry, spiritual drive, and material response to the needs of humanity in order to enthrone peace among individuals, groups, communities, nations and the world.

We have also seen that the same drive to search for existential truth led him into the exposition of African philosophy through Igbo metaphysics, in which he defined the true nature of man as *mma-di*, "good that is". In this philosophy, the origin of human, "good that is," is the supreme "good in se" (God), and thus man derives his goodness by participating in the goodness of God. The combination of all these factors forms Edeh's social philosophy. Since the ontological nature of man, according to Edeh, positions man as an extension of his Maker "good in se", Edeh's social philosophy by extension prescribes the imperative of treating *mma-di* with dignity and love.

The next part of this work now delves into the Millennium Development Goals (MDGs) and Edeh's contributions in each of the eight MDGs. It needs to be emphasized that he has been working in this direction for average of one and a half decade before the MDGs were set. His work towards the holistic emancipation of humans from socioeconomic and spiritual impairment began fully in 1985, upon his return to Nigeria from the United States of America after his studies. Before discussing the specific ways that Edeh's social philosophy aligns with the MDGs, we will take a look at three important concepts of Edeh's social philosophy: Community, *Omenani* (tradition), EPTAism/ECPM.

2.1: Community in Edeh

Every human being lives in a society and human society is made up of communities. When Aristotle, the ancient Greek philosopher and one of the greatest thinkers of all time says that man is a social animal, he is referring to the need for man to live in society and the inability of individual humans to be completely self-sufficient. Aristotle sees society as good and a worthy place for the development and welfare of humans.

Logically, Edeh's notion of community is influenced by the Igbo thought pattern. His experience of the Igbo milieu shaped his sense of community and informed the philosophy set down in *Towards an Igbo Metaphysics*. In this traditional Igbo milieu, a community engenders the spirit of unity and brotherhood—evidence of interdependence between *mma-di* and the community. He says: "In an Igbo community which embodies traditional culture, there is cooperation among people residing permanently in a single locality. The members of such a community share the basic conditions of common life" (Edeh 1985, 56–57). This is the type of community where *mma-di* fares well, as people in society cooperate.

For Edeh, we ought to live in and cooperate with the community while we still maintain our personal identity. He notes that "the community strives to maintain the different groups within it while maintaining itself as a community. Hence, the life and purpose of the community come, in certain matters, before the individual interests of the members" (1985, 57). Thus, the community Edeh advocates is a community of interdependent human beings who accommodate one another to serve the greater good. Aristotle's view of man as a social animal seems to agree with Edeh on this point, as Aristotle sees man's growth and survival as dependant on his relationship with the society.

Mma-di contributes naturally to the community while the community aids *mma-di* and maintains the good in good that is. Edeh (1985) corroborates this point by stressing that in the Igbo traditional context, life and existence belong equally to the community of being formed by dead ancestors and to the people who are still alive. Above all, life belongs to Chineke, the maker, author, provider, and sustainer of life and existence in its entirety.

To stress the logic of Edeh's philosophical anthropology in its application to the achievement of world peace, Egbekpalu (2011) reasons that God, good in se, created all human beings to partake in His goodness; that every person, irrespective of colour, race, education, religion, or other differences partakes in the same ultimate destiny. Furthermore, since all people originate from God, everyone created by the same God should live harmoniously in the same world as a result of our shared origin.

In today's world, we have become highly constrained by artificial constructs including racism, ethnocentrism, nepotism and hatred, and these barriers are opposed to the healthy development of any society. Rather than work with a harmonious, brotherly, communal spirit in the philosophy of Edeh, some people, out of ignorance, have lost touch with their ontological realities, thereby jeopardizing the nexus with their final destination. Many other selfish people of the contemporary Age are trying to transmute themselves into lifeless, mechanical entities and demigods, in disharmony with the human status of good that is.

To overcome this negativity, we must nurture community as Edeh sees it: with the flavour of communalism and inspiration of Chineke, the origin of *mma-di* and author of the universe; and as a quest for an unbreakable existential unity of life, a communion of *mma-di* with society and the maker of the universe. Edeh's concept of community abhors individualism, since individualism truncates the unity and comprehensiveness of human life and the true nature of humans.

In Edeh's notion of communal existence, we see ourselves and the world at large as two inseparable sides of the same coin. In addition, we are dependent on society and morally obliged to help society. In this communal cohabitation, everyone is expected to uphold the integrity of the other to ensure the symmetrical welfare of all. As Egonu (2005) remarks, humanity must remind itself, in view of modern science and technology, of the sacredness of human life, the joy of living, the beauty of creation, and the responsibility of all to protect all, to cooperate to promote the common good.

2.2: Omenani in Edeh

Having seen Edeh's concept of community, it is now vital that we should bring the concept of *omenani*, or tradition, into the discourse. Africans in general live a group life, as reflected in extended family system, existence of various traditional social institutions, including age grades, women's groups, councils of elders, councils of titled men and village or town unions. The peculiarity of these groups lies in the strong ties that bind their members and the relationship their members have with one another and the larger society, coupled with the sacrifice members make for the sustenance of their groups and their effective use of these units as agents of socialization.

The Aristotelian affirmation that man is a social animal is once again evident in African worldview, bringing into light the efforts made by average African to preserve the community by establishing strong bonds with the nuclear family, extended family, social groups and the community in general, as these ties consolidate solidarity among members of the society. Africans are strongly attached to family and they believe that home is always the best, and the number of years they live in a foreign land in no way negates their ties to this origin.

For the Igbos of West Africa, the ties to home are so strong that when an Igbo man dies in a foreign land, his corpse must be sent back to his hometown and his father's compound, where he would be given a proper burial so that he may continue his journey with his ancestors. Even if an Igbo man lives oversees, he still makes financial and other material contributions to the sustenance of his home community. His separation by distance does not undermine his share of strong emotions for, obligations to, and attachment to his people.

Tradition is the entirety of relationships of a people and their cultural traits, attitudes, tendencies and lifestyle, transferred from one generation to another. No community exists without tradition and it provides the standards, norms, and values that define the people's ways of life. The Igbo community is patterned by Igbo tradition. Thanks to tradition, people are bound not only by biology but also, by social relationships, interdependence, and mutual expectations.

Edeh understands the importance of tradition in the Igbo worldview, noting that "community is structured the way it is on account of Igbo adherence to the stipulations of tradition" (Edeh 1985, 58), and this has also influenced his social philosophy. He knows that tradition is needed for a cohesive and peaceful society. *Omenani* is the Igbo term for "tradition," and it is a strong binding force for the Igbos. The fundamental question here is: what is the relationship between *omenani* and community? They are inseparable, since no community can exist without customs and tradition, but customs and tradition cannot exist without a particular human community. Edeh explains *omenani* in this way:

> Tradition by definition can mean an inherited pattern of thought or action, such as a religious practice or a social custom. It also means cultural continuity in social attitudes and institutions. The Igbo concept of tradition includes all these and more. The Igbo word for tradition is "omenani." It is also translated as "obibendi," that is, "according to what is accepted in one's community." "Omenani" comes from two roots, ome and ani. Ome denotes action, dynamic activity. It has the same root as "omume," which means action, act, conduct, doing. This in turn has the same root as *"omimi,"* which means mystery, depth (1985, 59).

In fact, to live in the Igbo community without the concept of *omenani* would be like living in a house without a strong foundation. In Igbo language, *ani* means land, ground, or soil and Edeh reminds us that the word is also used for the earth goddess, which the Igbos regard as the highest and most universal goddess in Igboland. In this direction, Ezechi Chukwu (2013) explains that earth (*ani/ala*) is a symbol of beauty and moral good according to Edeh and as a result, it is revered as a goddess in Igboland as it is in many other cultures. Thus, Edeh defines *omenani* as "an inherited pattern of thought and action customarily and mysteriously in harmony with the dynamic creativity of being with the totality of all that is" (1985, 59).

An important point here is that *omenani* connotes action—practices in consonance with the virtues and values of the land and the will of the earth goddess, the "terrestrial expression of Chineke, the all-embracing supra-sensory being" (Edeh 1985, 59).Thus, *omenani* is synonymous with order, concordance, justice, unity, and peace. *Omenani* is emblematic of the Igbos' shared ideals of what is just and right. It is a reminder to humanity that irrespective of ethnicity, colour, or geographical location, humans are ontologically the same; each person is like other people because of our ontological oneness even though we still maintain our individuality which renders every person unlike any other one.

The truth of the matter is that *omenani* gives meaning to Igbo life, which guarantees the people's survival and corporate unity. Edeh (1985) also explains that the spirit of *omenani* is always in accord with the sense of mystery and the supernatural with the idea of keeping all in tune with the community of being. *Omenani* therefore is in association with the sensory and visible as well as the suprasensory and invisible, all in relationship with the thoughts and actions of the people. This concept of the harmony of existence is consistently vivid, whether the people are thinking and acting as a community or as individuals. If Plato could describe the state as a family in the *Republic,* how much more the Igbos, whose social co-habitation is inspired by the spirit of *omenani? Omenani* gives the Igbos a sense of family, community, coherence, and identity.

Evil is in opposition to *omenani:* "Whether an evil is an offence against anyone or anything, whether it is an occurrence among the living, the dead or gods, the Igbos see it as a removal of an aspect of the well-being and completeness of '*omenani*'" (Edeh 1985, 104). Since *omenani* is an inherited pattern of thought and action that is mysteriously in harmony with the totality of all that is, Edeh furthermore elucidates: "As a clarification of this, we must add that, *omenani* is a generic term for the body of Igbo socio-religious laws, customs and traditions, passed from generation to generation and handed down to the ancestors from God, Chukwu, through the Earth-god. For the Igbos an evil is regarded as an offence against *omenani*" (Edeh 1985, 103).

Edeh (1985) makes it explicit that any breach of *omenani* is regarded as a breach of the peace and harmony of the community, which is likely to result in a tragedy for both the individual who made the error and the community. Since an individual lives in the community and cannot imagine his survival without it, the offence is treated as a community affair. Ezechi Chukwu (2013) remarks that the dignity of *mma-di* is also protected through *omenani*, therefore, any breach of *omenani* is equivalent to the desecration of the land and the perpetrator of the *aru* (evil) by implication de-*mma-dizes* himself as a result of the abomination.

He continues, "When, therefore, a person commits a societal or moral offense, he is in effect regarded as having severed himself from this closeness, thereby stepping outside, as it were, the spiritual substance of the culture and running the risk of not fulfilling himself as a person" (Edeh1985, 105). However, this spiritual substance of the culture was the intended legacy of the ancients, the founders of Igbo culture whose spirit accompanies *omenani*. Ifemesia (1979) remarks that the characteristic ways of life of the Igbos bring the Igbo communities into existence and also make it possible for them to actually survive, progress and establish their identity in the larger human community. Basically, one cannot disregard the role *omenani ndi Igbo* (tradition of the Igbos) has played in this process of the Igbo coming to be.

Omenani is actually the source of the people's cohesion and value; it is equally the pillar of their common good. Edeh says, "Man must form a union in order to enter into communion with other men in order to safeguard his own existence. This was the intention of the founders of Igbo society" (Edeh 1985, 106). Since man lives in the community, his actions are not done in isolation. He forms part of the wholeness of life and *omenani* does not allow him to break this existential unity that binds the living and the dead with the Supreme Being, Chineke, who cares for all and maintains divine order.

2.3: Edeh's Philosophy of Thought and Action (EPTAism) and Edeh's Charity Peace Model (ECPM)

We have seen Edeh's views on the concepts of community and *omenani* and his concept of *mma-di* as an ontologically autonomous being who realizes the fullness of his or her existence in the community. According to Edeh, humans participate in the divine good of their maker and ceaselessly depend on God's absolute creativity, greatness, care and love for all their earthly affairs. With the concept of *omenani*, the Igbos achieve harmony with what is and what ought to be. We must understand that we have our origin in the Absolute: "good in se" and from Him, we derive our nature on a participatory note as "good that is," *mma-di*. Because of this derivation of our nature from the absolute good, it becomes necessary that we treat one another well in both theoretical and practical terms. When this is done, peace will prevail and the good nature of humans will reign.

It is this desire for permanent peace that led Edeh to develop his Philosophy of Thought and Action (EPTAism). Since EPTAism is peace oriented, Edeh accordingly devised a model of peace to complement it: Edeh's Charity Peace Model (ECPM). A fusion of EPTAism and ECPM makes Edeh's mission of practical and effective charity concrete. We can understand the ECPM in this way: "It is a model of peace that is anchored in practical and effective charity. The practical and effective charity is further rooted in the philosophy of man (*Mma-di*) "good that is"; philosophy espoused by Edeh. The philosophy of *mma-di* finds its highest expression in the Supreme *Mma-di*" (Agbo 2012, 27). We can now see the inextricable unity of humans with God in concordance with the practical and effective charity of the ECPM. Emphasizes Agbo:

> The divergent views on different things: leadership, economics, social setting, religious confession, etc., constitute

the major cause of division, conflict and the like. However, good understanding of man shows that he is a holistic being, a microcosm. He is fully sufficient but effectively dependent. He is or has a spark of God, a sense of autonomy and indispensible need for heteronomy; and an inevitable manifestation of "theonomy". Man and woman, in a dialogic form gave birth to yet another man, making his individuality to be rooted in community. The community is an expression of God's work of creation, unity in diversity (Agbo 2012, 29).

Edeh's presentation of African metaphysical thought is not enough in his view, that is why he goes on to demonstrate a concrete and practical realization of that philosophy, thereby arriving at an interaction of thought and action. "Thus this is what can be called EPTAism that is, Edeh's Philosophy of Thought and Action" (Edeh 2009, 48). EPTAism also leads to an African concept of theology that God exists and humans lean on him for survival, something that Africans experience in daily life and form religious practices around.

Edeh (2009) explains that the need to present African philosophy as an ideal of human existence and human dignity, along with his life experience and his belief that all beings created by God are ontologically good, spurred his mission of practical and effective charity. To bring peace to the world, we must approach people without segregation or prejudice and Edeh's sense of charity embraces the downtrodden, the sick, the poor, the abandoned and the victims of social maladies. In short, Edeh's charity alleviates humans' ugly situations.

In the Igbo thought pattern, God, *Chineke*, not only creates but continues to be present in the creature. He is *Chi-ukwu*, the Big God and the Greatest *Chi* (God), for no greater chi could be thought of. God is also *Osebuluwa*, who cares, loves, supports and consistently caters to the needs of humans and aids us in the actualization of the ultimate end of our existence. Thus: "If God as *'Ose-buluwa'* cares and supports man to the realization of his purpose, I must care and support my fellow man to the realization of his purpose and this leads to peace in his heart, peace in the society and to the modern world" (Edeh 2009, 49). Edeh therefore believes that the next step is to concretize this endeavour through practical and effective charity.

Unfortunately, we have reached an age of civilization in which we have mistaken ourselves for God. Our accomplishments in science and advancements in technology have regrettably given us a sense that we have arrived by efforts devoid of any *supratemporal* intervention. This know-it-all ego has invariably created a gulf between us and our maker. The same loss of our sense of origin has contributed to the modern idea that man is a means, an object and an element, rather than an end, a subject and a person.

Wars, ethnic clashes, international conflicts, homicide, genocide and other forms of violence easily trace their sources in humanity's withdrawal from our Creator. If we lose our connection with Chineke, the "good in se," we also lose our own goodness, becoming void of our own nature, as a result we finally become *mma-di-less*. When *mma-di* is removed from Chineke, he automatically lacks the completeness of his being and in this case, acting in accord with his original state as good that is becomes impossible.

ECPM is a reinstatement of the authentic relationship between human and human and between human and God. In order to realize the essence of creation, we must be connected to the supreme good and our own *mma-di*. It is not sufficient to explain this verbally because this reality must be practiced and lived. Edeh's Charity Peace Model is the *practicalization* of our goodness in our relationships with others in other to achieve a genuine peace. The goodness of God is best acknowledged when man is treated as that which he is by nature, good that is. It is impossible for anyone to genuinely love God and venerate Him without extending care and love to others.

In his critical look at the concept of charity in the ECPM, Ezechi Chukwu (2013) gives it credit for being a model concerned with how one hearkens to reason as a conscientious moral agent by seeking the good of everyone. The deontological nature of human good and morality is important because it mandates us to "do good, perform practical charity because there is an intrinsic good in doing so" (Chukwu 2013, 33). Charity, according to Edeh, also goes beyond almsgiving, which is only of secondary importance.

> It is important to note that the concept of charity in Edeh is not necessarily alms-giving. Alms giving in Edeh is only on the second order. The first order is to recognize man simply as "good that is" (*mma-di*), irrespective of creed, colour, religion, social status, ethnicity and all other artificial

barriers. It is only when we accept this primordial reality shall alms giving makes reasonable impact. Edeh believes that you can only be genuinely compassionate to your fellow men when you realize that man is good by nature and by the same token deserves love. Hence the expression: practical and effective charity (Chukwu 2013, 33–34).

Edeh's form of charity is imbued with African philosophy, a lived philosophy, a philosophy of human experience with no room for duality between thought and action. This inseparableness of thought and action in Edeh's philosophy is evident in Edeh's Philosophy of Thought and Action (EPTAism), which has also developed into a school of thought. The moment we realize that God is the ultimate cause of our existence, we will have no option than to act in harmony with *mma-di*, as designed by God.

Edeh insists that man should wake up from his slumber and understand first that God is the ultimate cause of his existence and second, that his real nature as *mma-di* is divinely ordained by God in unity with his ultimate reality and the purpose of his existence. Man cannot run away from this fact because he cannot pretend that his being is purposeless. He cannot equate himself with lower creatures and abandon his exalted position as the king of the temporal realm in a permanent rapport with the Ultimate Good (God).

2.4.1: Millennium Development Goals (MDGs)

According to Wikipedia, the Millennium Development Goals (MDGs) are eight international goals for development officially established following the Millennium Summit of the United Nations in 2000, as a result of the adoption of the United Nations Millennium Declaration in which the MDGs were established. All the 193 member states of the UN and at least 23 other international organizations have agreed to achieve these goals by 2015.

The then UN Secretary General Kofi Anan set the stage for the MDGs in his famous paper, "We the Peoples: The Role of the United Nations in the Twenty-First Century," published in 2000. The Millennium Forum made additional contributions to forming the MDGs in collaboration with more than one thousand NGOs and civil organizations across the globe.

In a nutshell, the Millennium Declaration asserts that every human being has the right to fundamental human conditions, including freedom, dignity, equality, shelter, and food. Thus "this Declaration reaffirms collective values, including equality, mutual respect and shared responsibility for the conditions of all peoples. We must recognize that good documents and strategies alone are never enough to reduce poverty. To tackle the problem, concrete actions are necessary" (Ugorji 2009, 59–60). The MDGs, with a fifteen-year timeline for their achievement, were intended as a concrete Action Plan to include the following goals:

- Eradication of extreme poverty and hunger
- Achievement of universal primary education
- Promotion of gender equality and empowerment of women
- Reduction of child mortality rates
- Improvement on maternal health
- Combating HIV/AIDS, malaria, and other diseases
- Ensuring environmental sustainability
- Development of a global partnership for development

Each of the MDGs has a specific target and deadline for achieving it. Developed countries were to partner with developing countries for the realization of the goals and to facilitate this, the G8 finance ministers agreed in June 2005 to raise funds from the World Bank, the IMF, African Development Bank (AfDB) and to cancel the debts owed by the heavily indebted poor countries (HIPCs). With their debts canceled, the HIPCs could redirect that money to the goals of poverty alleviation, expansion of education and the improvement of health.

The cancellation of these debts that developing countries owed highly industrialized countries was significant, for such a debt is usually a threat to countries' development thereby rendering the plight of the indebted countries equivalent to neocolonialism. Such debts continue to widen the gap between poor and super-rich countries and if the world does not take drastic measures to reverse this trend, the gap will only widen further, leaving poor countries perpetually on the margin. Ugorji (2009) emphasizes the efforts of Pope John Paul II and other religious leaders to solicit for an extreme reduction or complete cancellation of the international debt burden to ensure equality between countries, to promote economic growth of poor countries and to restore the dignity and equality of all people in the new millennium.

Many government agencies have pledged their support toward the realization of the MDGs. In fact, most governments in Africa now provide for the accomplishment of the MDGs and international campaigns such as the UN Millennium Campaign and the Global Poverty Project have been formed to assist in the realization of the goals. The important question remains: to what extent have these efforts yielded the desired result?

However, there is much debate surrounding both the progress towards the goals and their attainability in general. One of the major points which analysts critical of the goals are saying is that progress is uneven. A major aim of the goals is to improve the social and economic conditions of the world's poorest countries, but some critics are of the view that the goals were set despite a lack of clear analysis of them. With a good part of the aid from developed countries going to debt relief, natural disaster relief, and military aid, one wonders what developmental impact such assistance could practically make. This also leads to an important question: To what extent have the goals actually been achieved?

2.4.2: Edeh: A Model of Poverty Eradication

An old saying goes that a hungry man is an angry man. No human being can survive without food and we need to nourish ourselves to maintain physical and spiritual equilibrium. Today, it is impossible to build an ideal nation without a good policy to tackle the problem of poverty and its related hazards. All components of nation building are useless if they do not work to eliminate hunger and poverty. This is why the United Nations set the elimination of extreme hunger and poverty as the first of the MDGs.

Fr. Edeh understands poverty very well. He knows that without food, *mma-di* suffers and becomes vulnerable to all kinds of biological and social vices. He also knows very well that the spiritual health cannot be achieved in isolation of physical and material needs, since man is made up of both matter and soul. The harmonization of thought with action, a key feature of African philosophy, is a driving force in Edeh's zeal to arrest hunger and poverty. In this vein, Fr. Edeh has established some schemes aimed at helping people earn a decent living and thus alleviate poverty and hunger:

Job Creation

A popular adage says that when you give a man a fish, he will eat for a day, but when you teach him how to fish, he will eat forever. Edeh believes that the best form of empowerment is to teach people how to permanently fend for themselves by creating employment opportunities for them. His organizations have given jobs ranging from unskilled to professional work to thousands of people in Nigeria and beyond.

Employment in Academic Institutions (Education Employment)

Onyewuenyi (2011) remarks that Edeh has more than twenty-two educational institutions at all levels throughout Nigeria. Obviously, these institutions are involved with human capital empowerment. Fr. Edeh's nursery, primary, secondary and tertiary educational institutions directly employ thousands of people and indirectly alleviate the plight of thousands more. The problem of unemployment has led youths to engage in thuggery, armed robbery, hired killing, terrorism and other social vices and it also leads to societal moral decadence, for an idle man is the devil's workshop.

Through these institutions, Edeh provides education, a basic instrument for the destruction of social cancer and creates employment for thousands of people, both from Nigeria and abroad. Future generation of Nigeria and other nationals who could have probably turned into social parasites are now empowered to participate in mainstream economic life and by empowering them, Fr. Edeh continues to bring peace to the world. The Vice Chancellor of Caritas University Amorji-Nike, Enugu, Prof. Lawrence Onukwube, gives us a tip of the iceberg when he states, "In Caritas University alone, Edeh provided jobs to over 600 people. In doing so, he has reduced the number of potential criminals by that number, thus bringing peace to the world" (2012, 93).

Onukwube's insight gives us a clue to the extent Edeh has gone to provide some people with a good sense of livelihood. Madonna University is twice the size of Caritas, with reference to their number of students and staff. Added to this are the staff and students of OSISATECH College of Education, OSISATECH polytechnic and the other numerous secondary and primary schools Edeh has established.

It is noteworthy that Fr. Edeh does not discriminate in his hiring. Onyewuenyi (2011a) observes that Fr. Edeh has over 25,800 people on his payroll across his establishments both big and small. In all his establishments, women have always been given equal opportunities as their male counterparts. Prof. Onyewuenyi who is the Deputy Vice Chancellor of Caritas University, affirms that 51.9 percent of that institution's labor force are male while 48.1 percent are female, showing us that Fr. Edeh is conscious of gender equality and thus strategically battles hunger and poverty through education employment.

Employment in the Health Sector

Fr. Edeh has created many employment opportunities in the health sector as a means of combating hunger and poverty. In the Madonna Teaching Hospital and in his other hospitals including maternity hospitals, clinics, science laboratories and paramedical establishments, many people earn a livelihood for themselves and for their families. Poverty is multidimensional and multi-contextual and that is why even when a medical doctor, nurse or laboratory technician is jobless, such a fellow is notwithstanding vulnerable to poverty.

In fact, when people lack the opportunity to better their lives and take care of their families, they easily fall below the poverty line and when a person is severely deprived of the fundamental human needs like food, shelter, water, education, and medical care, that person is poor. In addition, when a person is unable to effectively participate in society because he or she is underemployed, that person could become psychologically poor. For instance, a medical doctor who must work as a bricklayer as a result of lack of employment opportunities in his field could be poor in this way. Therefore, Edeh has provided opportunities for medical and paramedical experts to practice their profession and to enable them live dignified and happy lives.

Provision of Mini-Industries and Self-Help Projects as Antidote to Hunger and Poverty

As we would recall, Edeh's Philosophy of Thought and Action (EPTAism) goes beyond philosophical speculation and indicates that man needs to be engaged productively for a meaningful survival. Because people need concrete means of living, Edeh's philosophy led him to establish mini-industries in order to create jobs and obliterate hunger and poverty. These empowerment devices include some of the following industries:

- Mini factory for the production of clean table water in Elele
- Mini factory for the production of clean table water in Okija
- Mini factory for the production of clean table water in Amorji-Nike, Enugu
- Bakery and confectionary mini-industry in Elele
- Beverage mini-industry in Elele
- Cosmetics mini-industry in Elele
- Paint factory in Elele
- Toilet tissue factory in Elele
- Wine factory in Elele

Everyone knows that the problem of unemployment is more than a mere academic exercise and Edeh's action goes the extra mile to solve it by providing jobs in these mini-industries for the betterment of *mma-di* and to put end to hunger and extreme poverty. People also learn new crafts in these mini-industries and centers, then go out on the acquisition of the requisite skills and knowhow to establish their own individual businesses, thus further increasing economic opportunity.

Considering the whole chain of production from the acquisition of raw materials to the sale of finished products to the consumer, an enormous number of people's lives are touched daily by Fr. Edeh through these projects. Lady Maria Goretti Omeogo of Mayfresh Savings and Loans Bank says of the project: "Hundreds of people after training have established their own businesses and are today employers of labour. Such practical economic empowerment has brought hope, peace and general well-being to the beneficiaries and the Nigerian society at large" (Omeogo 2009, 103).

Employment in the Service Industry

Edeh's quest to exterminate hunger and poverty knows no bounds. With determination, his philosophy of charity has led him to institute the following media and service establishments and thus created many professional jobs:

- Caritas University Radio in Enugu
- Madonna University Radio in Okija, Anambra State
- Pilgrim International Newspaper
- OHHA Micro Finance Bank
- Our Saviour Printing Press, Agbani Road, Enugu

Caritas Radio is an employer of labour and also a voice of moral education and academic excellence for the society. The same is also true of Madonna University Radio, Orkija. They are radio stations with a difference: In addition, they inspire morality and propagate the message of love, hope, brotherhood, proper citizenship, and of course, the philosophy of charity and peace which their founder, Emmanuel Edeh, has lived for all his life.

OHHA Bank also has many workers on its payroll from unskilled cleaners to top bank managers. At Our Saviour Printing Press, too, many people have jobs that enable them to be financially independent, thereby overcoming the menace of poverty.

Employment in the Catholic Prayer Ministry

It is no longer news that the site of the Catholic Prayer Ministry, founded by Fr. Edeh in 1985, is today a National Pilgrimage Center (National Shrine). Its elevation to this status by the papal nuncio to Nigeria in November 2012 was an epoch-making event. The National Pilgrimage Center of Eucharistic Adoration and Special Marian Devotion, Elele is the fifth largest Catholic pilgrimage center in the world and the first in Africa. Thousands of people go there on daily bases to worship and to pray to God for their needs. God has blessed many people through this ministry and testimonies of miracles abound there. The ministry also employs a lot of people, including cleaners, clerks, secretaries, curators (in the museum), security guards, salespeople and shop attendants etc.

Poverty Eradication through Educational Empowerment

While we observe that Edeh employs a lot of people in his education establishments and thus raises their living standards, his efforts to combat hunger and poverty through education do not end there. He also uses the education itself to uproot hunger and misery from the lives of his students and graduates. To live in this modern Age without proper formal education is to live without access to vast opportunities. It is difficult to imagine what life must be like, in this Age of technological advancement for a youth who for instance has no rudimentary knowledge of computer.

Through education, Edeh has empowered and continues to empower thousands of youths, thereby extricating them from the brink of penury and removing the chains of hardship from them. In Edeh's schools, students acquire professional knowledge and skills that will enable them to enter the labor market upon graduation. The courses offered in these schools include but not limited to the humanities and law, nursing, medicine, laboratory science technology, food science technology, natural sciences, engineering and theology etc. Graduates from Edeh's institutions excel in various sectors and different countries of the world where they work and by so doing, they become asset to the Nigerian nation and global community.

Edeh is convinced that through education and compassionate care, peace is instilled in people's hearts and that if the rest of the modern world could absorb this philosophy of compassionate caring, then rancor, restiveness, kidnapping, murder and of course hunger and poverty would be things of the past; as peace would reign in the human heart and society.

The famous slogan for Nigeria, "Good People, Great Nation," is fantastic, but it is a mere fantasy if citizens, especially young citizens, are not empowered with an education that would enable them to realize their potentials. Poverty cannot be eradicated through almsgiving alone. Hunger cannot be annihilated if youths are not trained so that they could unlock the latent greatness in them. In a nation without good education, life is like the Hobbesian state of nature—solitary, poor, nasty, brutish, and short. But just as important, education without morals is like empowerment without moderation. In Edeh's institutions, education is ornamented with morals, which leads to a balanced *mma-di* and desirable citizenship. With this feature, there is always increased demand for his graduates.

Provision of Scholarships

As a way of practicing EPTAism, Edeh has given scholarships to various categories of students to enable them graduate and live a happy life permanently above the poverty line. Edeh believes in hard work and he encourages excellence. He is convinced that it is a sin if children and youths are not motivated to virtue, diligence, hard work and greatness. To this end, his schools offer scholarships to students who show outstanding academic performance.

We recall that Edeh's notion of humans as *mma-di*, "good that is," derives from his creator and he is therefore permanently good because of this divine origin. In this understanding, anything that does not aid the full manifestation of his true nature is abhorrent and *anti-omenani*. Also, in this African concept of humans, it is an abomination to think of abandoning handicapped people, for to do so is to deny an authentic person of his or her authentic nature. Thus, as a way of giving them a sense of what they are, *mma-di*, Edeh created a special scholarship to enable them study and to empower them to bid adieu to extreme hunger and poverty. Many of such people have graduated from OSISATECH polytechnic and are now the breadwinners of their families.

Edeh also offers scholarships to other students in difficult circumstances. Among his students are those who encountered financial constraints and thought they would have to abandon their studies before graduation. However, Fr. Founder, as he is popularly called, awards bright and disciplined students scholarships so that they do not have to leave because they cannot afford the school fees. Parents appeal to him when it seems impossible for their children to continue with their studies and in his large heart, coupled with his notion of charity and the feeling of moral responsibility towards these students, Fr. Edeh usually offsets the school fees of students whose financial woes are genuine.

Work-Study Opportunity

Sound morals demand that workers should have the opportunity to grow and employees are therefore truly empowered when, in addition to a good job and salary, their employers give them opportunities to develop professionally. Fr. Edeh has always encouraged his staff to further their studies while they work and a good number of his staff members have acquired higher academic degrees while they work.

Many who came into their employment in Edeh's institutions with diplomas now have first degrees, those who had first degree can now boast of having master's degrees and some of the tutorial staff who started with master's degrees even hold doctorates today. To facilitate this advancement, his workers are given easier admission to Edeh's universities and polytechnics than others. Through this practice, Edeh, in an indirect way, further empowers his employees and saves them from the menace of poverty.

Edeh also offers a work-study program for those students whose parents or guardians cannot afford the school fees. Onyewuenyi (2011a) says that such students work within the institution and receive wages for their services, enabling them to defray the full cost of their education. Thus, Edeh gives them the opportunity to continue with their education and have a brighter future.

Empowerment to Host Communities of Edeh's Establishments (Corporate Social Responsibility)

Every great organization should attract development to the community in which it is established and Edeh is fully aware of this corporate social responsibility. In fact, as a way of empowering the communities where his establishments are located, he gives their local youths scholarships. His schools themselves also attract infrastructural development to the communities. Some of these communities have enjoyed roads with good access only since Edeh's institutions came there. For example, the village of

Elele was relatively unknown, but thanks to Edeh's work, Elele has become a household name in Nigeria today. The presence of such institutions usually leads to the opening of various business enterprises by mainly the indigenes of the host communities around the institutions.

Empowerment through Job Security

Every worker dreams of a permanent job. To ensure job security in Fr. Edeh's institutions, he believes strongly in providing equal employment opportunities and hiring on merit—he conducts key interviews himself and assesses the interviewees without discrimination. When they are hired, most members of Edeh's staff are employed permanently. It is then up to them whether they wish to continue work or to resign if they so desire. With such job security, these staff members are empowered both materially and psychologically.

Empowerment of Those in Umuogbenye (Poorest of the Poor) Rehabilitation Center

No individual has the capacity to employ all the job seekers in any country. Either because of laziness, natural or man-made circumstances, some people cannot fend for themselves. Some of these people end up as loafers and wanderers. Due to such ugly circumstances, they can neither afford shelter nor feed themselves. Many of them have neither a basic education nor knowledge of a craft. They are a liability to both their families and the state. Fr. Edeh still considers them as his fellows and as *mma-di*, who desire love, care, food, and shelter. On the premises of the Catholic Prayer Ministry in Elele is a large neighborhood called Umuogbenye (poorest of the poor) quarters, where Edeh harbors these poor people of God. He accommodates these hundreds of people, providing food, shelter, access to medical care and even rehabilitative services for them.

As far back as 1986, Fr. Edeh established Our Saviour Rehabilitation Center in Elele for the reorientation and reintegration into society of youths who had posed danger to the society. In this way, Edeh succeeds in disentangling the poorest of the poor from the disaster of hunger and consequently converting them to valuable members of society.

MDGs Assessment: Eradication of Extreme Hunger and Poverty

Target: Reduce the proportion of people whose income is less than one dollar a day to half the 1990 level.

Progress Report

Without doubt, poverty is one of the causes of social vices such as armed robbery, juvenile delinquency, ethnic tension and war. Hunger and poverty also damage individuals' health. Therefore, poverty also keeps people from realizing their life goals and prevents all people from achieving peace. The UN's efforts to reduce extreme hunger and poverty therefore require the participation of everyone. In the paper: "Restoring the Dignity of the Poor in Nigeria through the Millennium Development Goals," during the theological convention at the Pilgrimage Center Elele, Nigeria: the Catholic Bishop of Umuahia Ugorji says: "If peace is to be sustainable in Africa, there is the need to address the high incidence of poverty which insults the innate dignity of the human person in the continent and reduces millions of people to a life of untold hardship and undeserved misery" (Ugorji 2009, 57).

The *Millennium Development Goals Report 2012* shows that the United Nations has made progress toward MDG Number 1: Eradication of Extreme Hunger and Poverty. However, this progress does not mean that there are not also challenges. In the report, UN Secretary General Ban Ki-Moon emphasizes that the target of reducing extreme poverty by half has been reached, ahead of the 2015 deadline, and that the problem of global shelter has improved commensurately.

In line with these affirmations, the UN Undersecretary General for Economic and Social Affairs Sha Zukang confirms the Secretary General's standpoint; as he also states that there is a clear reduction of poverty in all of the world, including sub-Saharan Africa. The report further notes that the world has met the MDGs target of accessibility to clean drinking water. In addition, it points out a remarkable improvement in the lives of the world's millions of slum dwellers, even ahead of the 2020 deadline for that goal. All of these mean that the problem of reducing hunger and poverty has been reasonably addressed within the ambit of the MDGs. **http://mdgs.un.org/unsd/mdg/Resources/Static/Products/Progress2012/English2012.pdf** (pp. 3 - 5).

The *MDGs 2012 Report* actually demonstrates that the world really made progress towards MDGs Number 1: Eradication of Extreme Poverty and Hunger. However, the exercise is still not without its challenges. Although these results validate the modus operandi of the MDGs, the UN should not relax, since the whole exercise is a continuing process.

In the report, Ki-Moon also remarks that based on projections, in 2015, more than six hundred million people worldwide will still be using unimproved water sources, while almost one billion will be living on an income of less than $1.25 per day. He also notes that the menace of hunger is still not over. Undersecretary General Zukang adds that inequality adversely affects efforts toward the MDGs. He reiterates that achievement of MDGs on the Eradication of Extreme Hunger and Poverty is unevenly distributed across regions and countries of the world (UN MDGs Report, 2012).

To this end, Egbutah (2009) sees agriculture, the foundation of food production, as the pillar of the effort of MDGs Number 1: Eradication of Extreme Hunger and Poverty. He makes it clear, however, that the actualization of this goal would meet a brick wall unless authorities intensified efforts to increase food production. In this way, we may also make efforts to increase food security, the accessibility to enough food and healthy nutrition for all people at all times so that they may live an active, healthy and worthy life.

This is in line with the affirmation that "the most effective strategy for making steady, sustainable progress towards the MDGs by 2015 is to stimulate the interests of younger generation in agriculture by emphasizing more dynamic, functional and practical methods in the teaching of agricultural science at all levels of our education" (Longshal and Usman 2009, 36).

Hunger remains a worldwide challenge that surely hinders both personal and societal growth. In the case of Nigeria, Egbutah further describes the relationship between agriculture and food security thus:

> The revitalization of the agricultural sector is very essential,
> if the economy is to be brought back on track. This is

because agriculture when properly practiced and supported has the capacity to achieve the objective of food security. To this effect all stake holders should put their hands on the deck to ensure that the problem of food security is greatly minimized, if not eradicated. Government is advised to provide good governance and demonstrate her political will, by injecting adequate funds and providing the enabling environment for food production and food security to thrive (Egbutah 2009, 27).

The *MDGs 2012 Report* relates in addition that those in vulnerable employment have decreased, although it emphasizes that the reduction is only marginal (UN 2012). The danger here is that those who fall in this category may resort to social deviances since they are unpaid or underpaid for their labour. This is a critical challenge which needs to be addressed in order to avoid among others, the exploitation of workers by their employees.

Recommendations from EPTAISM

The Philosophy of Mma-di: Understanding the true nature of humans as "good that is" is an important step to the solution of human problems. It is when people are accepted within this context of divine origin that policy makers at the local, national, and international levels will make effective laws and policies that improve human welfare.

Continuous Job Creation: Edeh continuously creates jobs as a weapon for combating poverty and hunger, and he continues to explore available avenues in which he can invest to create more jobs for families, thus putting an end to their hardship. The MDGs should likewise be focused on the angle of job creation because without the continuous creation of employment, the problems of poverty and hunger would continue and the MDGs Number 1 would continue to suffer a setback.

Continuous Provision of Good Drinking Water: Water is a necessity for human existence and Fr. Edeh is fully aware of this. This is why he has strategically embarked on projects to produce clean drinking water to serve all his organizations. However, no individual can provide water for the whole world, so the United Nations should partner with indigenous governments of the world in a bid to provide drinking water for all communities and thus prevent waterborne diseases like typhoid and cholera.

Provision of Shelter: In Edeh's institutions, students are entitled to full accommodation and a good number of staff members, both faculty and non faculty, are also given accommodation in Elele, Orkija, and Akpugo etc. Edeh believes that any human being without shelter is already poor, so he provides accommodation in order to create an enabling environment for his staff and their families.

Incentive to the Disabled (deaf, dumb, blind and crippled): These people have no voice in the *MDGs Report 2012*, so we do not know to what extent the United Nations has developed a specific work plan to accommodate them in our society. Can the MDGs Number 1 be said to have genuinely made progress when this group is not particularly considered? In this regard, the UN can learn from Fr. Edeh, who has an action plan for the integration of disabled people into the society for the benefit of all. As already mentioned, he provides a scholarship for them at OSISATECH polytechnic and he engages them by giving them the opportunity to learn crafts at his mini-industries and other employment schemes.

Commitment to Employment on Merit: Many people today are poor not necessarily because they cannot work but because they are victims of discrimination. Mma-di in Edeh means that all in the human community are the same. When people are discriminated against, they get frustrated and dejected and can become antisocial.

Poverty as a result of racism, nepotism, tribalism and gender inequality are all evil in the sight of the Creator, *Chineke*. The United Nations should also consider how to address this type of poverty caused by unnecessary discriminations in the society. Edeh sets standard for different categories of workers irrespective of where they come from. Nobody is denied access to opportunities in his organization as a result of racism or favoritism. To do so, the MDGs could be structured to encourage parity in employment opportunities, in different sectors all over the world; coupled with hiring based on merit, as evident in Edeh's methods.

2.4.3: Edeh: A Model of Education for All

Academic Institutions founded by Edeh
- Madonna University, Okija, Nigeria(1999)—the first private university in Nigeria and the first Catholic university in West Africa
- Caritas University, Amorji-Nike, Enugu (2004)
- OSISATECH polytechnic, Enugu (1989)—the first private polytechnic in Nigeria
- OSISATECH College of Education, Enugu (1989)—the first private College of Education in Nigeria
- Saviourite House of Formation (senior seminary), Enugu
- 5 secondary schools
- 3 primary schools
- 3 nursery schools (kindergartens)

Scholarship Programs at Edeh's Institutions
- scholarship program for the handicapped
- work-study program
- scholarship for academic excellence
- scholarship for indigent youth
- special scholarship programme for the physically challenged
- special scholarship program for host communities

Scholarly Publications (Books) by Fr. Prof. Edeh
- *Towards an Igbo Metaphysics*, 1985. Translated into Italian, Spanish, French, and the Igbo language.
- *Peace to the Modern World*, 2006.
- *Igbo Metaphysics: The First Articulation of African Philosophy of Being*, 2009.
- *Authentic Catholic Theology*, 2008.
- *Edeh's Charity Peace Model*, 2012.
- *The New Philosophy: At the Service of Truth*, 2011.

- *University Cooperation: Experiences in Founding Catholic Universities*, 2011.
- *Qualitative Catholic Education as the Basis for Meaningful Development as Evident from Blessed Pope John Paul II's Proposals1995–2005*, 2011.

Publications Edited by Prof. Edeh

- *The Church of Jesus the Saviour in Africa,*vol. 1 (Lineamenta), 2009. Organizer and editor.
- *The Church of Jesus the Saviour in Africa*, vol. 2 (Instrumentum Laboris), 2009. Organizer and editor.
- *The Catholic Prayer Ministry and the Pilgrimage Center of Eucharistic Adoration and Special Marian Devotion, Elele*, 2004.
- *Madonna University: An Institution with a Difference*, 2004.
- *God the Father the Beginning and End: Tertio Millennio*, vol. 2, 2008.
- *Jesus the Saviour in Our Midst: The Third Millennium*, vol. 1, 1998.
- *The Holy Spirit Acting in Our Midst: The Third Millennium*, vol. 2, 2000.
- *The Pilgrimage Center of Eucharistic Adoration*, 1997. Edited with I. K. B. Ngwoke.

Some of the Scholarly Books Published Exclusively about Edeh

- *The Mustard Seed of Jesus the Saviour in Elele,* by R. N. Onyewuenyi, 2009.
- *Authentic Human Development: Insights from the Metaphysics of Rev. Fr. Prof. Edeh*, edited by Onyema Uzoamaka, 2009.
- *African Philosophy: Contemporary Trends*, edited by Stephen Ojobor, 2009.
- *Aspects of Edeh's Philosophy*, vol. 1, edited by C. B. Nze, 2011.
- *Aspects of Edeh's Philosophy*, vol. 2, edited by Ezechi Chukwu, 2011.
- *Actualization of the Millennium Development Goals: Fr. Edeh as a Pacesetter*, edited by Ezechi Chukwu, 2013.
- *Edeh's Charity Peace Model (ECPM)* First and Second Edition. Edited by N. N. Chukwuemeka, 2012.
- *Fr. Emmanuel M.P. Edeh: Inspiring 21st Century Africans to Serve First*, by P. Amah, 2012.

- *The Dignity of Man in African Metaphysics as Epitomized in EPTAISM,* by M. Melladu, 2011.
- *Servant-Leader Emmanuel M.P. Edeh: An Inspiration in Youth Empowerment & Poverty Alleviation: The Nigerian Experience,* by R. N. Onyewuenyi, 2011.
- *Peace to the Modern Society: A Short History of the Father Founder Very Rev. Prof. E.M.P Edeh CSSp. 2004. By Mother John Bosco Kalu, SJS*
- *Fr. Edeh Before the Journalists. Editor Barr. Emeka Okpala, 2011*
- *Responses to the Questionnaire on Very Rev. Fr. Prof. Emmanuel Mathew Paul Edeh CSSp, OFR. Editor Rev. Sr. Dr. Purissima Egbekpalu SJS, 2011*
- *A short Profile of Very Rev. Fr. Prof. Emmanuel M.P Edeh CSSp, OFR, 2010, By Albert U. Ogbodo PhD*
- *A short Biography of Very Rev. Fr. Prof. Emmanuel M.P Edeh CSSP. OFR, 2011*
- *By Zulu Adigwe*
- *Biodata of a Legend of our Time: Very Rev. Fr. Prof. Emmanuel Mathew Paul Edeh CSSp., OFR. By Fr. Josephat Emeka Ezenwajiaku FJS, 2011*
- *Man and Peace in the light of Edeh's Philosophy of thought and Action. By Assoc. Prof. Remy Onyewuenyi CSSp, PhD 2012*

Edeh has founded educational institutions to better the lot of humans and in Fr. Edeh the Catholic priest, there also exist Prof. Edeh the teacher, scholar, researcher, and author. As a result of his amazing contributions to education and the practical improvement in the realities of human existence, students and researchers today investigate Edeh's life and espouse his thought for the benefit of the academic world and humanity at large.

The large number of papers on Edeh presented regularly in academic and religious institutions enrich the intellectual community. Furthermore, those articles, books and other publications facilitate the development of African philosophy in particular, human development and aid the cultivation of global citizenship in general. In Edeh's words: "It is obvious that when every person lives one's nature as 'good that is,' the echo of *mma-di* would transverse humanity because man sees himself in the being of others, his goodness in the goodness of others, and peace would eventually reign in the world" (personal interview by the author with Edeh, March 15, 2013).

The Madonna University International Convention of Experts and Intellectuals, an annual five-day rendezvous of intellectuals organized by Madonna University in Nigeria, usually attracts accomplished scholars and experts around the globe to inform participants about the life and philosophy of Edeh in general and the practical application of his philosophy in various contexts around the world. Many scholars for instance discuss his philosophy of *mma-di*, which is neither selective nor discriminatory. His pioneering work and masterpiece, *Towards an Igbo Metaphysics*, earned him an award in 2011 as an articulator of African philosophy of being from the prestigious University of Nigeria Nsukka.

Edeh has made a landmark achievement in education. His desire is to use education in addition to academic excellence to recognize and position man genuinely as *mma-di* in all people and thus consolidate the ontological nature of human as "good that is" who is in permanent cohesion with his Creator. Edeh's academic centers, which are all founded on sound moral principles, are designed as formative institutions that respond to the material and spiritual needs of humanity, unlike most other contemporary institutions of learning, which are purely concerned with academic performance. Ebo confirms:

> It is reasonable to argue that formal education, that is the type of programmed instruction and knowledge imparted in designated centres according to conventional criteria, taken in isolation, can never encompass the significant range of forces that go to the shaping of the individual personality. A complex organism, the human individual is an amalgam of forces from diverse sources that incessantly impinge upon him and condition his feelings, memories and perceptions. Formal education is a major source of these formative influences. Other equally significant sources are less structured (1989, 30).

The need to blend formal education with the "less structured" significant forces of formative influence, including the nonmaterial and the supra-temporal, led Edeh to develop a curriculum of all-round education for the comprehensive development of man. For instance, at all his tertiary academic institutions students must attend a three-hour orientation once a week that includes two hours of physical exercise and then moral instruction. Irrespective of his tight schedule, Fr. Edeh dedicates time to partake in this exercise, as he considers physical exercise to be an integral habit for the well-being of the students and the larger society.

The first executive president of Nigeria, Alhaji Shehu Shagari, delivered a paper titled "Education: The Greatest Investment for Development" at the convocation of Bayero University, Kano, on January 16, 1982, in which he said the following of education and development:

> Education must enhance *Political, Personal and Social development*. Man must be taught political awareness and knowledge of civic responsibilities. Education must ensure democratic and human ideals and an even and just distribution of resources and social amenities like schools, hospitals, shops, markets and factories, without tying these up with party politics. Education must foster a sense of unity and nationalism. It must produce selfless political leaders who are objective and non-tribalistic. It must allow personal development. Man must preserve his social identity by way of religions, traditions and customs, respect for one's heritage brings with it a sense of security. Science and health education must enhance the quality of human life and fight dirt, pollution, destitution and delinquency (Shagari 1982, 67).

It was as if President Shehu Shagari had read the mind of Fr. Emmanuel Edeh when presenting this paper, even though Edeh was in far away Chicago as a researcher. Fr. Edeh returned to Nigeria two years later and since then, he has made monumental strides toward accomplishing all of those points Shagari raised in that address. From fostering poverty alleviation to education, health to youth empowerment, social justice to religion, cooperation to unity, charity to peace, Edeh has stood tall among his contemporaries. Edeh's God-man-world scheme as evident in Igbo metaphysics underpins that no society can be truly human without morality and sense of responsibility. According to Edeh (2009), this scheme gives credence to the dignity of human being and human existence.

As a way of matching words with action in the education sector, thereby affirming the *ime* (doing) part of African philosophy, Edeh began establishing institutions of learning in the mid-1980s. Edeh had the need to nurture his fellow humans as authentic *mma-di* and as world citizens at a time when education in Nigeria was almost comatose.

Life is faced with difficulties and these challenges remain as we advance both individually and collectively. However, because we are rational beings, these chokepoints should only stir us to greater efforts to improve on what we have, allowing our one talent or endowment to become two. We as individuals and our governments have a great responsibility to teach such a philosophy to youth and thus put them on the path of learning for life. Edeh believes strongly that the mind of every human being needs to be instructed and improved with education and religion.

The learning environment should promote students' growth by providing suitable support for acquiring skills and learning proper behaviour, attitudes, and values. Education is vital for the fullness of *mma-di* and the importance of the learning environment towards that goal should not be underestimated. In that regard, Edeh (2006) insists that the achievement of African philosophy, which values holistic care for all as members of one family, could not be realized without good education. Edeh recalls the devastation of the Nigerian Civil War of 1967–70, which led to the near total collapse of the educational system in the country and giving way to myriad of institutional vices like exam malpractice, campus violence, and academic decay in general (Edeh, 2006).

Consequently, thousands of helpless youths ended up as armed robbers, killing and destroying human lives and properties. It was in the face of the above circumstances that Edeh struggled from 1989 till date to establish different categories of government certified tertiary institutions for the provision of quality education and moral excellence. Today, these institutions: OSISATECH Polytechnic, OSISATECH College of Agriculture, Madonna University and Caritas University Enugu are all citadels of good education.

The ancient Greek pre-Socratic philosopher Heraclitus (circa 500 BC) who says that fire is the origin of all things also says that permanence is an illusion, as all things are in perpetual flux. Following this Heraclitan dictum, the founding of Edeh's tertiary educational institutions restored confidence in education in the country. Parents and guardians sent their children to his institutions, where they received good education and where there is the absence of those social ailments that had previously devastated the educational system.

In order to relieve parents of the burden of school fees especially the poor and the handicapped, Edeh instituted extensive scholarship programs in each of the institutions he founded. Dr. Mike Ike Okwudili, the Rector of OSISATECH polytechnic, testified that Edeh's institutions were established to transform Edeh's thought into reality and that Edeh has provided academic and moral education in these institutions. He stresses that Edeh's scholarship programs provide for the disabled and abjectly poor, thereby transforming the lives of many students who had been a burden to society. Dr. Okwudili goes on: "Worthy of mention is the case of Agbakuribe Bamidele, a blind man who benefitted from Edeh's scholarship scheme who is now a lecturer in the University of Abuja. He is currently pursuing his Ph.D. and is happily married with children" (Okwudili 2011, 159). Many such beneficiaries of EPTAism consequently add value to society.

Former Deputy Vice Chancellor of Madonna University Orkija, Assoc. Prof. Ngwoke (2006), remarks that Fr. Edeh can be summarily described as a person whose desires have been modeled through his continuous self-sacrifice for peace, reconciliation, rebuilding of shattered lives and restoration of lost hope. Since 1984, Fr. Edeh has been strenuously engaged in the arduous tasks of pairing his philosophy with action not only by himself but also and above all, through his educational institutions.

In his assessment of Edeh's academic institutions, Unegbu (1996), the former Vice Chancellor of Caritas University, says that Edeh established a good number of "humanistic institutions" that cater to the various needs of mankind:

> In his human development efforts, he has established Our Saviour educational system that operates at all levels: namely, primary, secondary and tertiary. His preoccupation for the welfare of the abjectly poor, the handicapped and the less privileged in the society has propelled him to establish full scholarships for any member of these groups that qualifies and gains admission into any of these levels (2006, 75).

Unegbu (2006) further relates that in these educational institutions, Fr. Edeh has set out to correct the evils and institutional anomalies that for years plagued the entirety of the Nigerian educational system and made it a source of ridicule, including secret cultism, campus unrest, strikes by staff and students, examination malpractices, imposition of the purchase of handouts on students, sorting, and sexism. In Edeh's academic institutions, in contrast, there is no room for these ills which bedevil education in Nigeria therefore, they are exemplary institutions.

Prof. A.U. John Kamen (2006) describes the Nigerian education industry before Edeh joined it as being in "shambles" and that "the state of education was nothing to write home about. Incessant riots and strikes among students or staff ravaged the educational system. In1997 for instance, apart from Fr. Edeh's OSISATECH Polytechnic and OSISATECH College of Education, all the tertiary institutions in the country were on strike for almost one full year" (82). It is easy to see the difference Edeh's institutions make.

Unegbu (2006) goes on to explain that through these institutions, Edeh has uplifted the abjectly poor and benefitted numerous troubled youths through his scholarship programs, thereby contributing to both human development and the betterment of society. Edeh is therefore, a reformer of education, his knowledge of *mma-di* and his inventiveness, love, dedication, and charity have enabled him to achieve monumental change in academia, thus fostering genuine peace in the world.

In addition, Ezechi Chukwu (2013) takes the stance that Edeh's institutions are dedicated to the teaching of moral values, thereby encouraging global citizenship among the students. Chukwu opines that some of these ingredients of EPTAism should be adopted by the United Nations for the smooth and effective implementation of the MDGs, especially in education.

Target: Ensure that, by 2015, children everywhere, boys and girls alike, will be able to complete a full course of primary schooling

Progress Report

The *MDGs Report 2012* shows that, against all odds, some progress is evident towards achieving parity in primary education for boys and girls, with girls seeing more benefits, and improvement in sub-Saharan Africa, compared with figures before the MDGs were set. The Report emphasizes that enrollment rates for children in primary schools have increased and that rates of children out of school have decreased (UN MDGs Report, 2012).

This achievement is encouraging since education is the pillar of human development and that is why it is enshrined in the MDGs. No matter a person's area of endeavour, education nurtures that person and gives him or her sense of direction in all his or her undertakings. Education equips us with skills, knowledge and the wherewithal to optimize our potentials, be effective in our career and fully actualize ourselves. Education is so important to human development that all countries of the world have their own policies for it.

Emphasizing the importance of education as key to the actualization of the MDGs, Mfam (2009) discusses vocational education in particular, noting that in both the private and public sectors, when employees have the right skills, obtained through the proper education, administrative efficiency is achieved, productivity improves, the economy of both the nation in question and the world definitely improve. Thus: "To achieve productive work for youth as envisaged under the MDGs, requisite industrial and employability skills and vocational competencies should be part and parcel of the learning experiences offered to students" (Mfam 2009, 21). In addition, vocational educational programs enhance employment opportunities, entrepreneurial know-how and managerial capacity of women, who are currently behind their male counterparts in employment.

To this end, "vocational-technical education is indispensible in the attainment of MDGs" (Mfam 2009, 22). While the achievements of the UN's goal in education is commendable, the UN is encouraged to intensify its efforts towards MDGs Number 2 and all stakeholders should collaborate to meet this goal, for education teaches not only skills and general knowledge, but it also imparts value to humans, gives them morals and breeds good citizenship both at the local and international levels.

The aim of MDGs Number 2 should be combined with the educational aims of the United Nations' Educational, Scientific, and Cultural Organization (UNESCO), which was founded in 1946 as an autonomous and permanent intergovernmental organization and agency of the United Nations. Its primary function is to foster peace and security among nations through education, science, and culture. It also advances universal respect for justice and the rule of law, human rights and freedom for all peoples of the world. With UNESCO's help, the propagation of mutual knowledge through worthy education and the cooperation of nations could be easily realized.

The French thinker Maritain (1943) remarks that the teaching of morality should take fundamental position in schools. The ancient Greek philosopher Plato also believed that genuine philosophical knowledge is the knowledge of the immaterial transcendent forms that are true reality. One of the central themes of Plato's concept of knowledge and education is the benefit of acquiring knowledge for its own sake. This informs Plato's philosophy of education and sociopolitical philosophy in general which attribute the leadership of the polis to the philosopher king who has a commensurate knowledge for the administration of the body politic.

The acquisition of knowledge, whether it is in terms of military tactics or public administration, requires rigorous effort by the individual. No doubt, this commitment is worthwhile because education is an integral component of human development. This is why Plato makes a clear distinction between the Sophist and the philosopher:

> The Sophist takes refuge in the darkness of non-being, where he is at home and has the knack of feeling his way, and it is the darkness of the place that makes him so hard to perceive … Whereas the philosopher, whose thoughts constantly dwell upon the nature of reality, is difficult to see because his region is so bright, for the eye of the vulgar soul cannot endure to keep its gaze fixed on the divine (Plato 1969, 999).

The progress towards achieving MDGs Number 2 is not smooth in every sense of the word, as the UN Under Secretary General for economic and social affairs remarks in the *MDG Report 2012* that the achievements were unequally distributed across regions and countries. A typical example of this inequality is evident between sub-Saharan Africa and Southern Asia. It is reported that in 2010, sub-Saharan Africa had a 24 percent of children of primary-school age out of school and Southern Asia reported 7 percent (UN MDGs Report, 2012).

The report further notes that there is in the world generally, a reduction in girls' exclusion from primary education, but a disparity in the improvement exists between regions and countries. Further on enrolment, there is also a danger that some pupils who register for primary school may not complete their studies due to financial constraints which though vary from one region to another. The need to complete primary school also points to the need for more secondary schools, as they may not be available in some areas due to economic limitations. Poverty also makes it difficult or impossible for families to send their children to school, just as more urban children attend school than those in rural areas (UN MDGs Report, 2012).

In short, the children who cannot go to school remain disadvantaged and have a bleak future. The MDGs should be rechanneled to close these gaps in access to education. When this happens, education will lead to development. Since development is all about human enhancement and in turn, enhancement of society in general, the achievement of MDGs Number 2 must be prioritized and the world should work hard in this direction. Chibueze (2009), in citing UNESCO 2008, relates that the international resolution to meet the 2015 target on education might be unattainable due to the poor learning outcomes in languages and mathematics across the world.

It is undeniable that progress has been made towards the MDGs regarding education. However, a lot more needs to be done, as we have seen. To accomplish this, we can borrow some ideas from Edeh, who has made astonishing success in education.

Adoption of the Concept of Mma-di: The United Nations should consider Edeh's concept of humans as "good that is" in the formulation of its education policy. Until the world comes to realize that all humans are ontologically good as a result of their origin, it will be difficult to achieve comprehensive education. The world needs care and love and Edeh provides them before anything else to his pupils/students and his concept of charity requires them, for without care and love; discrimination, maltreatment, indifference and social disparity will continue unabated.

Absence of Gender Discrimination: As a way of filling the gap between enrolment of male and female students, gender is not a condition for admission in any of Edeh's schools, which have given access to education to thousands of people from different parts of the world. Because of his notion of *mma-di* and his concept of charity, he has created in these institutions enabling study environments, despite the great cost it imposes on him, so that many African youths and Nigerians in particular, may realize their dreams of having good education and a fulfilled life.

Thousands of the youths who attend Edeh's schools could have ended up on the streets had it not been for the efforts of the ordinary priest and teacher, Emmanuel Edeh. Onyewuenyi (2011a) notes that these institutions have offered education of undoubted quality to "over 53,000 youths" and this number continues to grow annually as students graduate. On the issue of gender parity in admission and educational opportunity, Onyewuenyi observes that this problem has already been solved in Edeh's institutions and that the gap has been filled already.

Of the students who matriculated in Caritas University in Enugu between 2007 and 2010, more of them were female than male. Onyewuenyi states: "Of the 2,331 who matriculated during the period, 1,195 (51.3%) are female while the remaining 1,136 (48.7%) are male. This is a change; a phenomenon to watch. It can be inferred from these figures that Fr. Edeh is not just offering the youth University education but equal University education opportunity" (Onyewuenyi 2011a, 57).

Merit as the Condition for Admission: The only condition for admission into Edeh's institutions is merit, not gender, a quota system, bribery, nepotism, or favoritism, for these illicit conditions inhibit academic progress and the optimization of human knowledge, for they discourage excellence.

The Inculcation of Moral Values to Students: Another important factor that the MDGs seem not to have considered is the moral disposition of graduates. Education is human formation and if we pay attention only to the technical aspect of academic knowledge at the expense of the moral and spiritual facets, the system would only produce mediocre citizens imbued with mechanistic and anthropocentric conception of man. This is another pillar of education in Edeh, a situation whereby formal education is blended with sound moral values.

Aid to the Less Privileged: In the *MDGs Report 2012*, the UN did not give the details of how the handicapped and less privileged in society have fared in education or whether any provision has been specifically made for them in the goal. However, Edeh has made a provision for them. At OSISATECH polytechnic as earlier mentioned they are offered scholarships to enable them have access to tertiary education. The UN should follow suit, otherwise handicapped people will be permanently left behind.

Quality Schools from Nursery to University: The UN should also partner with various national governments to provide quality schools for students and pupils across the globe at all levels, especially in third world countries in order to accommodate the teeming global population, following the example of Edeh, who provides good quality schools from nursery to the university level.

Completion of Academics: It is not enough for the UN to consider only the enrolment of male and female students in MDGs Number 2. Whether they finish their studies is just as important. In Nigeria, for instance, industrial action by lecturers and sometimes on-campus violence by students have often led to the elongation of students' academic careers by additional one or two years. This disheartening situation, however, does not exist in Edeh's institutions. In all of Edeh's academic institutions, courses of study always fit within the timeframe of the school calendar and students graduate by the date stipulated as the official end of their courses.

Security: Unfortunately, student cultism festers in most academic tertiary institutions in Nigeria of today. These organized criminal enterprises made up of students mastermind terror to their fellow students, lecturers and school staff. It is not clear whether the MDGs have considered this inhibitor to education. An academic institution ought to be a citadel of knowledge and not an incubator of gangsterism. To prevent this type of activity, Edeh provides accommodation with twenty-four-hour security measures in all his tertiary institutions. Except during holidays, students leave campus only by permission after indicating the purpose of their exit, thus keeping students and staff safe during this period of vulnerability.

Welfare: In addition to adequate security, Edeh increases student welfare by providing clean water, electricity and recreational facilities etc.

Religious Tolerance: *MDGs Report 2012* does not indicate the extent to which the MDGs have ensured the free integration of students of divergent religious backgrounds into the academic environment. However, Edeh's institutions have a strategic lesson to teach: although they are Catholic institutions, they are also open to students and staff of other religions, as they are communities of *mma-di* and therefore do not engage in religious discrimination. Christians of different denominations are entitled to their beliefs and to worship as they wish and so are Muslims and members of other faiths.

Discipline: Another important characteristic of Edeh's institutions is the rigorous enforcement of discipline for both staff and students for the common good. Lecturers are made to attend classes at the appropriate time and to structure their courses following school ordinances and assess students' examinations objectively. Students are required to attend lectures and do their assignments and their adherence to these rules is continuously assessed. Furthermore, undisciplined activities like the viewing of obscene films and other erotic materials are completely outlawed in Edeh's institutions. Violent and unruly acts like fighting, stealing, and sabotage are met with severe punishments.

These are some of the strategies Fr. Prof. Edeh successfully employs in his educational institutions that the United Nations should emulate to realize MDGs Number 2. Most parents who send their children to Edeh's schools today do so because of these innovations. Knowledge is power and the good use of it is more powerful. For the development of any nation, promotion of education must be on the front burner. Edeh's philosophy of *mma-di*, with its practical application through EPTAism, has transformed education in his institutions and it can be hoped that it will take the world far if it is adopted as a means to implement the MDGs Number 2, especially in Africa and the third world in general.

2.4.4: Edeh: A Model of Sustainable Health-Care Delivery

Health Institutions and Initiatives founded by Edeh

- Our Saviour Hospital and Maternity, Elele, 1986
- Our Saviour Rehabilitation Center, Elele, 1986
- Our Saviour Motherless Babies Home, Elele, 1992
- Our Saviour Specialist Diagnostic Laboratory, Enugu, 1991
- Our Saviour Specialist Diagnostic Laboratory, Okija, 2001
- Madonna University Teaching Hospital, Elele, 2002
- Caritas University Medical Clinic, Enugu
- Madonna University Medical Clinic, Okija
- Our Saviour Pharmacy, Elele.
- Free medication for Bishops and advanced Priests
- Healthcare for the indigent
- Rehabilitation Center for the Mentally Retarded
- Madonna University Medical Clinic, Akpugo

Health is wealth, for an unhealthy person cannot perform optimally. Edeh's 2006 book, *Peace to the Modern World* has two major semantic purposes: first, to provide Fr. Edeh's declaration to serve humanity and second, to give testimony of the concrete and self-evident practicality of that declaration. In that piece, Edeh posits his mission of practical and effective charity, reiterating his commitment to care for all the people of God, including the insane, needy, sick and downtrodden.

As part of his mission to instill peace in humanity, Fr. Edeh established the public health-care delivery schemes listed above to cater to the health needs of *mma-di*. Edeh states, "For the healthcare of the abjectly poor and abandoned it became imperative to found a number of medical institutions to bring healthcare to the doorsteps of the thousands in the society who cannot help themselves" (2006, 11). These initiatives demonstrate the immense value Fr. Edeh assigns to human life, which is no surprise in light of his notion of humans as "good that is."

Edeh does not want to leave any category of *mma-di* without proper care and love and he always desires to bring peace to everyone, therefore he has founded the various health-care delivery schemes listed above, for he knows that illhealth strips human potential as well as human life.

Amah (2012) states that Edeh is convinced that people's intrinsic potentials, if harnessed properly, will enable them to rise above their limitations. Edeh therefore maximizes everything within his reach to lift people from the shackles of illhealth and empower them to bring about the best of themselves. To accomplish this, he spends time in consultation with those who bring their multifarious needs to him. He does not allow them to go unless he has given them the attention, care, and love that they deserve. Since God, Osebuluwa, cares for man, Edeh believes that we should care for *mma-di* by showing all love and providing for their good health. Peter Amah summarizes Fr. Edeh's efforts thus:

> From my interviews and observations, it appears Edeh is not necessarily the voice of the voiceless as much as he is, on a small scale, the food to the hungry, clothes to the naked, home to the homeless, healing to the sick, hope for the hopeless, courage to the weary, shelter to the orphans, peace to those in conflict. He plays these and many other virtuous roles, sometimes on a large scale, because of his faith in and desire to emulate Jesus the Saviour. He is a man with goals who is giving, humble, and result-oriented (Amah 2012, 33).

Edeh is committed to the healing of all sicknesses, both physical and spiritual. As Amah's interviews reveal, Edeh plays out his "virtuous roles" on a large scale because of his faith in Jesus the Savior and his passionate desire to emulate him.

Edeh's health-care initiatives began with the establishment of Our Saviour Hospital and Maternity Center and Our Saviour Rehabilitation Center in 1986, fourteen years before the official inception of the MDGs.

Edeh then founded a home for motherless babies in 1991 and since then, this center has been giving succor to numerous children who may have otherwise died.

The reduction of child mortality is the fourth MDG and Fr. Edeh's health establishments alleviate not only the sufferings of the poor but also work squarely beyond that. As already emphasized, he started this even before the MDGs were set, as an expression of Edeh's mission of practical and effective charity, to better the lot of others through selfless efforts.

Nwoye (2013) observes that Edeh does not allow abandoned children to be relegated to lives of penury and hunger and this is underscored by Edeh's establishment of Our Saviour Motherless Babies' Home. He gathers these children, makes them feel at home, as they would feel in their parents' homes and eventually facilitate the realization of their life dreams because they are *mma-di*.

Edeh makes these selfless contributions to humanity in the pursuit of peace without announcement. Amah (2012) says that he was attracted to researching Edeh's leadership style because of Edeh's humility and preference to hide behind the fame of Jesus rather than to achieve personal media coverage. Amah relates that in his personal interactions with Edeh, the clergyman has emphasized that his primary interest is to inspire and influence people's lives.

Edeh therefore sees himself as a mere instrument of God to enable *mma-di* to actualize his good nature and as a mere messenger whose work cannot overshadow the original sender of the message, author and principal actor, Chineke. Praise, according to Edeh, is for God only and not for man. We can see then that Edeh works for the power of love rather than the love of power.

In some countries today, especially third world, malaria, typhoid and measles are still major killers. The scourge of malaria is a global one. The World Health Organization initiated the Roll Back Malaria (RBM) program in 1998 to stop the agony of this disease. The RBM summit, which was held in Abuja, Nigeria, in the year 2000, sought to enhance the anti malaria fight in Africa and the choice of Abuja as the venue indicates the problem this epidemic poses not only to Africa but also more specifically to Nigeria which is the most populated country in Africa and the largest black nation in the world.

This summit sought to reduce malaria-related deaths in Africa by at least half by the year 2010 with a combination of preventive and curative measures. These measures in question include the use of insecticides and treated mosquito nets and efforts to keep the environment clean. While WHO's efforts have been commendable, it is still unfortunate that malaria remains a major killer in the third world, especially in Africa.

Since 2000, the year of the Abuja summit, malaria has not yet become a thing of the past. It is still responsible for a relatively high proportion of world deaths annually and Africa remains at high risk, with malaria the most endemic parasitic disease on the continent. With malaria, along with cholera and HIV/AIDS ravaging humanity, especially in Africa, one wonders about the sustainability of health promises and policies made by various local and international institutions.

In "Edehization of the Millennium Development Goals," from *The Actualization of Millennium Development Goals: Fr. Edeh as a Pace Setter,* Ezechi Chukwu (2013) observes that malaria, typhoid and measles continue to hold sway as child killers. Furthermore, child mortality caused by malnutrition and lack of access to drugs is still pronounced. However, Chukwu (2013) emphasizes that Edeh has played a prodigious role in the reduction of child mortality in his endeavour.

Thus, with his multiple health-care schemes, including hospitals, clinics, departments of medicine and Nursing in his universities, scientific laboratories and courses on environmental studies at his universities, Fr. Edeh continues to provide a strong theoretical and practical panacea to the scourge of child mortality. Many children who are treated daily in his hospitals would have probably died had they depended only on public health-care institutions. In addition, Edeh continues to make wonderful contributions to improved maternal health and combating HIV/AIDs and other diseases, thereby using the machinery of EPTAism and ECPM to save lives and bestow peace to the human community.

Edeh's philosophy of *mma-di* is manifested in this area, as his continuous struggles to combat HIV/AIDS and to improve on maternal health by and large conform to the African philosophy of being that he developed. For example, a lot of poor expectant mothers receive free treatment in his facilities and HIV/AIDS patients often receive free drugs and these efforts are in agreement with Edeh's mission of practical and effective charity.

MDGs Assessment: Reduction of child mortality rates:

Target: By 2015, reduce the mortality rate of those under five by two-thirds of the 1990 level.

Improvement of maternal health:

Target: By 2015, reduce the maternal mortality rate, by three quarters of the 1990 level.

Combating HIV/AIDS, malaria, and other diseases:

Target: By 2015, have halted and begun to reverse the spread of HIV/AIDS.

Progress Report

The *MDGs Report 2012* states that progress on the child mortality front has been made, and according to Sha Zukang, UN Under Secretary General for economic and social affairs, child survival progress is gaining momentum. There has also been an increase in the treatment of people suffering from HIV/AIDS in the whole regions. The measure to halt tuberculosis is yielding positive results, while deaths as a result of malaria are also being reduced. While the proposed decrease in maternal mortality rates is still far from the 2015 target, there has been improvement in that regard and in maternal health (UN MDG Report, 2012).

Health is wealth, but an unhealthy person lacks the capacity to realize the fullness of his or her existence. In this regard, the positive results towards MDGs Numbers 4, 5, and 6 is good news, although the UN should improve on its Action Plan to achieve more effective global healthcare and governments at all levels should also be mindful to provide health programs to achieve these three MDGs.

In the paper "Science Education and the Achievement of the Millennium Development Goals (MDGs) by 2015," Garba (2009) states: "Very often, efforts to attain the MDG target can inadvertently meet with some challenges. Therefore, there is no simple solution to the problem. It is more productive to understand that a dilemma exists between, on one hand, efforts to achieve the MDGs and on the other hand, efforts to overcome these challenges" (14). Garba further observes that inconsistency in policy formulation and proper coordination of programs could mar institutional administration and policy implementation where it concerns the MDGs.

The fight against HIV/AIDS is a common battle and malaria in particular is a major human killer in sub-Saharan Africa. To concentrate on poverty eradication without giving proper attention to health is to generate counterproductive measures. We must institute vigorous campaigns to prevent these deadly diseases while also putting in place adequate curative measures. The world is an integrated union like the human body, so what affects one part affects the other. Therefore, the whole world must make concerted efforts to achieve good global human health. Mfam explains:

> HIV/AIDS not only affects the individual, it touches entire communities and countries. As more and more teachers die from HIV/AIDS, children are robbed of an education. Farmers dying of HIV/AIDS are unable to provide enough food for their families and villages, causing more poverty and hunger (2009, 20).

Although there are new drugs that can prolong life for HIV/AIDS patients, there is no drug that can cure this disease so far, therefore we must intensify effort mainly on prevention. People all over the world should be encouraged to embrace formal and sex education; although illiteracy and ignorance do not directly cause diseases, but one cannot deny the fact that illiteracy is a barrier to receiving information about healthcare and behaviours that prevent disease. In this vein, it is imperative that the UN should not be left alone in this battle for world health. Nations, NGOs, civil society organizations, corporations, international organizations, and religious institutions should all contribute to this important quest to enthrone adequate human and environmental healthcare for all.

Irrespective of the general progress made in the health sector, there are still some challenges as evidenced in 2012 UN Report. While Northern Africa for instance has achieved the MDGs target on the Reduction of Child Mortality, on the other hand, Sub-Sahara Africa and Oceania the Report says have achieved only less than half of what is required to reach the set target. In this case, mortality rates for the under-five is still a challenge, just as there is the need to resume progress in the reduction of measles-related mortality as agreed by World Health Assembly in 2010.

It is also noted that the 2015 target on maternal mortality is still far from being realized. Above all, while access to treatment by those who live with HIV has increased, sub-Saharan African on the other hand is left behind (UN MDGs Report, 2012). If these trends are not reversed, the socioeconomic progress of the individuals, families, countries, and regions concerned and by extension, the world in general, will be hampered.

All the eight Millennium Development Goals are intertwined and it is therefore difficult to target the realization of any of them in isolation. For example, maternal health affects child mortality, because the health of a pregnant mother impacts the health of her baby in the womb. Partnership and cooperation are needed to tackle the menace.

It is true that biomedical technologies for screening, scanning and provision of therapy improve maternal health and reduce infant mortality, but such technology does not guarantee the extermination of these problems. Further, the scourge of HIV/AIDS is still very much alive, irrespective of the public sensitization to its effects by media coverage and the efforts of various institutions.

The challenge of the HIV/AIDS pandemic calls for a comprehensive global reappraisal involving individuals, families, religious organizations, health-care workers, and educators. In this vein, Dabo and Msheliza (2009) call for a guide to avoiding illicit sexual relationships. While families should be deeply involved with the socialization of their children, religious organizations should take up the task of providing their moral grooming. Furthermore, health institutions should partner with the educational sector to organize sensitization workshops and seminars and to hold classes on the causes and effects of HIV/AIDS in schools.

Man as *Onye* (Person) Rather than *Ife* (Thing): In his explanation of Igbo metaphysics, Prof. Edeh (1985) makes a systematic inquiry into the Igbo notion of being and describes human being as more closely linked with *onye*, "who," rather than *ife*, "thing/object." For Edeh, *Onye* in the Igbo grammatical syntax: "unquestionably conveys the idea of a human being" (Ibid: 94).

Edeh lays emphasis on the fact that *onye* can be used as a noun: "In this category, it is nearest but not the exact English equivalent of person" (Edeh 1985, 94) and can also be used to refer to other living entities that are superhuman. The peculiarity of *onye* in this context is that even when it is used as a noun, it normally precedes a noun or an adjective: for example, *Onye nwe*? ("Who is the owner?") and *Onye nwe uwa* ("The owner of the world"). Edeh further explains that *onye* conveys the "idea of human being" and that it can be employed to "designate spiritual beings."

In continuation of his analysis, he makes it explicit that the term, '*being*' more generally cannot be designated with *onye*:

> In no way can one stretch the Igbo concept of "onye" to embrace things like stones, wood, or iron, etc. If, for instance, a piece of stone fell and broke a plate, an Igbo person would ask, "Onye kwuwalu afele?" (who broke the plate?) "Onye" here can never refer to the stone. What it refers to is *who*, the person who dropped the piece of stone that broke the plate. Hence *Onye* is not comprehensive enough to translate the term *being* (Edeh 1985, 94).

This principal defect of *onye*—that it is unable to denote nonhuman and non spiritual entities—places a dichotomy between the animate and the inanimate. Whereas *onye* has an inbuilt link with the human and animate, *ife*, on the other hand, has a direct link to things. Edeh continues, "The Igbo word *ife* primarily means *thing*, anything material or immaterial. It is also used to refer to a happening, an event, an occurrence. *Ife* can be affixed to any adjective or a verb to mean a specific thing" (1985, 95).

In this regard, it is clear that while a human could be designated with *onye*, he could never be defined as mere *ife* only, for *ife* cannot designate a human being. While we can ask, *Kedu ife bu ihe a?* ("What is this thing?") about objects, we can only say *Onye bu onye a?* ("Who is this person?") for a human. Edeh's health-care programs put this duality between animate beings and things, subject versus object, principal versus attribute, mainstream versus ephemeral, and, of course, *mma-di* as "good that is" into consideration.

Healthcare in Edeh, whether it works toward MDG Number 4, 5, or 6, considers humans as *mma-di* and as onye, not as mere ife. This thoughtfulness is key to Edeh's health-care approach. Edeh concludes that "human beings are the principal focus of the visible world" (1985, 97). Therefore, his health-care services approach each of those they serve as *onye bu mmadu* (one who is good that is) and not as *ife nkiti* (a mere thing or object).

Campaign against Premarital Sex: The *MDGs Report 2012* states that access to treatment for people living with HIV increased in all regions, to the extent that at the end of 2010, 6.5 million people were receiving antiretroviral therapy for HIV or AIDS in developing regions. However, the report states that the 2010 target of universal access had not been reached. The fundamental question here is that even if the target were reached, is the approach of the MDGs to the prevention of HIV/AIDS viable? Does MDGs seek to condemn premarital sex?

Edeh condemns premarital sex since it degrades the sexual relationship, which is tied to the union between husband and wife. We recall that in Edeh's concept of *omenani*, anything that is at variance with omenani is anti-omenani as a result, is *aru* (abomination), which usually attracts the expression *tufiakwa* (forbidden). Edeh believes we therefore need to discourage the abuse of sex in this way, especially by youths. These youths will understand the purpose behind this discouragement when they are at the period of biological and social maturity. By doing so, we drastically reduce the potentiality to new infections of HIV/AIDS. Prevention is better than cure, as the saying goes. To reach the MDG target of reduction is one thing, but to discourage it in practical terms and consolidate on the achievement is a different thing altogether.

Discouragement of Sex and Sexism on Campus: Unfortunately, the UN report on MDGs does not take into account the various environments and circumstances in which people and young ones in particular, easily contact HIV/AIDS. With the sense of liberty and maturity that students claim in secondary and tertiary educational institutions, many of them are disposed to engage in sex. They are away from the direct influence of their parents or guardians and this is the age at which they rebel against institutions, authority, and standards. Therefore, they approach sex with recklessness and are exposed to contacting HIV/AIDS and other venereal diseases and this is responsible for the proactive measures adopted in Edeh's institutions.

Discouragement of Illegitimate Sex in General: As a reflection of African philosophy, which is more practical than abstract, Edeh is a crusader against illegitimate sexual relationships. Edeh is opposed to clandestine sexual relations because it could easily lead to many health hazards and gross unethical practices. It is obvious that unwanted pregnancy, especially for non married partners for example is usually vulnerable to abortion, mainly if the baby is rejected by either or both biological parents on account of illegitimacy, inability or non preparedness for the baby and this could be morally wrong. Thus, can lead to the willful extermination of fetus. How then do we classify this kind of mortality?

There are cases where unmarried ladies and teenagers get pregnant, give birth to the baby and subsequently abandon the child due to lack of commensurate means of sustaining the baby. This is even equivalent to infanticide and is therefore totally condemnable. Youths are today carriers of venereal diseases and HIV/AIDS more than legitimately married couples because of this laxity towards sex. Is it not better to take a proactive measure as Edeh proffers?

EPTAism, a harmonization of theory and action, condemns all indiscriminate sexual relationships and Edeh outlaws them in all his institutions, both academic and otherwise. Edeh insists that it is better that we avoid those conditions that lead to diseases and other ailments instead of opting to cure them. Students are human beings who are vulnerable in an environment in which they have no direct supervision from their parents or guardians, therefore Edeh guards them so that they and their families and society do not fall victim to the consequences of illicit sex. This is one important area that the UN should reflect on for the realization of MDG Number 6.

Love to Victims of Sickness: Another important area that the UN's *MDG Report 2012* did not address is the way that victims of various ailments are catered to and shown love by government authorities. To what extent do governments and other authorities treat them as *mma-di*? Do governments seek to treat them as human beings loved by their Creator, Chineke? Do they ensure that against all odds, the sick are not discriminated against? To what extent are they given a sense of happiness and spiritual renewal? These are the questions Edeh's philosophy answers and his facilities work to implement.

Through his prayer ministry, which is now a National Pilgrimage Center, Edeh gives thousands of people hope and joy irrespective of their state of health. He makes them understand that their tribulations have not in any way taken away their ontological status as "good that is" and loved by their Creator. MDGs in the area of health-care should therefore be targeted also at showing practical love and kindness to patients.

Responsive Health-Care Initiatives: Edeh prefers prevention to cure, but he also provides measures in case the preventable is not prevented. He uses all his medical establishments and health-care programs to continuously combat child mortality and HIV/AIDS, malaria, and other diseases. He also uses them every day to improve maternal health. Above all, Fr. Edeh uses his health initiatives to revitalize the poor, the downtrodden, and the abandoned living in our midst, often treating them for free.

2.4.5: Edeh: A Paragon of Gender Parity and Women Empowerment

The question of gender equality has taken center stage in the global discourse in the past few decades. Since antiquity, we have lived in a male-dominated world. The *Oxford Advanced Learner's Dictionary* defines *gender* as "the fact of being male or female," but there is clearly more to it than that. It poses theoretical concerns and generates a lot of ethical questions as well. For instance, are men and women different and what do they have in common? Do gender issues intersect with other systems of inequality? Is there really a complicated imbalance between the genders in society? Do we still live in a patriarchal society? Are females truly suppressed and discriminated against in every sector of life and every institution? If so, are people working to correct this imbalance?

In short, the issue of gender is surrounded by a myriad of complex questions, but the truth of the matter is that man and woman are ontologically created equal by the Creator. However, the sexes do exhibit different biological features. The individuals who produce sperm cells are generally classified as male, while the individuals who produce egg cells are classified as female. Thus, the biologist conceives sex and the sex of a particular individual as being grounded in reproductive processes.

One of the fundamental characteristics of living organisms is their ability to reproduce themselves and this can be done in two ways. The first is the process of asexual reproduction in which part of the organism in effect breaks off from the whole to form a new individual. Amoeba is one organism that reproduces in this manner. In asexual reproduction, the genetic material of the new individual is identical to that of the original organism.

The second type of reproduction, the method that human beings use, is sexual reproduction, in which a new individual is formed from the genetic material contributed by two separate members of the species. This process has the advantage of allowing for greater variability among members of the species and thus a greater chance that they will survive to pass on their genes. For this type of reproduction to happen, the cells that contain the separate sets of genetic material must merge with each other.

When this occurs, the new organism must be nourished until it is sufficiently developed and the egg cell provides this nourishment. The other reproductive cell, called sperm, only penetrates the egg cell and contributes its genetic material. Once this happens, all things being equal, a human male or female is born as an individual whose life is as valid as any other.

In any case, the meaning of *male* and *female* in everyday life is quite different from their biological and reproductive sense because, while male and female distinguish each other for the purpose of reproduction, not all people can or wish to reproduce and with the help of new technologies like artificial insemination and embryo transplant, human reproductive methods have changed.

Edeh believes that both male and female share equally the status of *mma-di*, "good that is," given to them by God, who is by nature the absolute good. Edeh states: "I maintain that the Supreme Being, Chineke, is the one who creates and remains present in his creatures, Osebuluwa is the one who cares and supports all beings to realize their purposes. The logical implication here is that God did not only create the world and abandon it but carries it along" (Edeh 2012, 3–4). To achieve world peace, he recommends African philosophy articulated through Igbo metaphysics, for "this can be achieved when men begin to see man (good that is) as created in the image of God and therefore deserves respect and care" (2012, 4).

These statements from Edeh show that he does not consider the genders to be unequal. He believes that both men and women are products of their Creator, who cares for and provides for them. He is therefore intolerant of discrimination by sex, as it is an offence against both God and humanity. Edeh describes the ideal of human dignity without gender, ethnic, or cultural bias and anchors it in the interplay between thought and action typical of African philosophy.

According to Edeh (2009), the philosophy of ideal human dignity gives people an ideal human existence. The ideal human dignity in question is based upon the believe that all beings created by God are ontologically good, and therefore, deserve respect. Every human being, whether male or female, is given a position of honor, prestige, and inviolable rights because together, they are the principal creatures of the Creator, Chineke.

Edeh is therefore, at the forefront of gender parity and this can be seen in his work even before the MDGs were instituted. In Igbo metaphysics, he developed the God-man-world scheme, which gives a strong foundation to the dignity of human beings and human existence in general. As he states: "African metaphysics is saying that we should accept man as good within the context of creation" (Edeh 2009, 40).

Today we talk of "natural rights" which are immutable, inviolable and universally applicable, irrespective of gender or other differences. These rights, too, show that men and women share ontological parity. However, this is different from a kind of justifiable social inequality, a situation whereby some people occupy privileged positions in families, organizations and institutions as a result of the rules, regulations and norms that guide them. Sometimes, some positions, ranks and cadre are necessary for bureaucratic and administrative purposes but all these should not undermine the ontological equality of all.

Edeh did not say that humans should be considered within the context of gender or any other artificial barrier but purely as "good that is," *mma-di*, participating in the order of the supreme good in se, that is God. The concept of "good that is" is neither selective nor discriminatory. The good that is knows no race, culture, color, or location of origin. The "good that is" considers not gender but upholds man and woman as ontological equals in the presence of their maker, Chi-ukwu. To say that man is *mma-di* is to say that woman is *mma-di*. Edeh strongly believes in this reality and works assiduously to treat everyone according to his or her merit rather than his or her gender.

While making a thorough assessment of Fr. Edeh's life and leadership style, Amah (2012) describes Edeh as a man who values people, a man who develops people, a man who builds community, a man who displays authenticity and a man who provides leadership and shares leadership. Amah remarks that because Edeh's thinking and actions are in accord with his concept of mma-di, he therefore makes the valuing of people an integral part of his vocation, understanding that the goodness in every human person must be sustained. Edeh also continues to develop people since every *mma-di* is naturally invested with potentials deserving of development to full realization.

The ongoing analysis makes it clear that Edeh does not hide his passion for fair play, equality and justice when it comes to gender related issues. The number of women he has integrated into the administration of his programs and institutions lends credence to this claim. In his institutions, women have been employed not only on professional merit but also at the highest levels of the bodies they work for. In Edeh's academic institutions, for instance, women hold principal positions such as headmistress, principal, Head of Department, and Dean of Faculties. In the nonacademic sector, they have risen to the level of accountants, administrators, and managers.

In Edeh's institutions at large, women have benefitted immensely and continue to benefit. In some cases, the level playing field Edeh has created has made women surpass men in their accomplishments. As Onyewuenyi (2011a) points out, the matriculations of Caritas University students between 2007 and 2010 demonstrate that female enrollment in the school is not only on par with that of males but has, surprisingly, surpassed that of males. This is concrete evidence of the empowerment of women at Edeh's institutions and a just way of institutionalizing gender parity without shortchanging these women's male colleagues.

MDGs Assessment: Promotion of Gender Equality and Women Empowerment

Target: To eliminate gender disparity in primary and secondary education, preferably by 2005, and in all levels of education, no later than 2015.

Progress Report

In developing countries, parity has been achieved in primary schools, irrespective of the fact that some regions are still backward, according to *MDGs Report 2012*.The good thing about this achievement is the fact that it could easily lead to equal opportunities for women in the sociopolitical and economic world.

In setting the MDG to bridge the gap of gender inequality, the UN has advised the entire world to make such efforts, which should be evident in increased job opportunities, political participation, professional duties, remuneration and all other areas of human endeavour. Gender equality must be seen as a human right in order to eradicate discrimination. In the paper "Democracy, Human Rights and the Commonwealth in the 21st Century: An Overview", Bourne (2004) states that the Commonwealth secretariat has an effective gender unit, which works in concert with the nongovernmental Commonwealth women's network. Bourne goes on to condemn the discrimination against women in some countries.

Gender disparities emerge in various ways in the education system, as noted in the *MDGs Report 2012* and unless these imbalances are corrected, they may unfortunately become permanent. The report emphasizes that girls face more bottlenecks at the secondary level of education than at the primary level due to discrimination in families and in societies.

The report also states that girls from poor homes are faced with the barriers to education compared with their peers from well-to-do homes. To complicate issues, women still have no access to jobs in some regions, and women are left to resort to informal means of earning a living. Further, even though women continue to gain representation in parliaments, it is still worrisome that the pace is relatively slow, although the situation is generally better there than in appointed positions in the executive arms of government (UN MDGs, 2012). However, it is still necessary that we treat every human being based on merit and not gender.

All socio-cultural inhibitions to the development and emancipation of women need to be dismantled and all socially constructed disabilities and artificial barriers used to discriminate against women need to be jettisoned, for such disabilities are sometimes used to achieve selfish ends. Reisine and Fifield (1988), whose work discusses the concept of disability and health status, state that contrary to the way disability is defined by bodies offering social security, the notion of disability is better understood by the historical definition of the World Health Organization (WHO), which says it is not only the absence of pathology but also social, physical, and psychological functioning.

The WHO goes on to differentiate impairments, disabilities, and handicaps, saying that a disability is a physical phenomenon, whereas a handicap is a culturally defined impairment. While disability refers to a restriction or lack of ability to perform normally, handicap means disadvantage due to impairment or disability.

Meritocracy: A Hallmark of Women Empowerment: According to the *MDGs Report 2012*, women do not have equal access to job opportunities as men in some regions, but Edeh provides men and women with equal opportunities in his employment. As emphasized earlier, Edeh defends hires based on merit, not gender. Amid claims and counterclaims that we live in a male-dominated world, Edeh has taken it as a responsibility to give women the positions they deserve, enabling them to rise to positions at the highest levels of his institutions.

Provision of Education for Women: To ensure that women have the opportunity to develop their potentials, Edeh provides education to girls and women from nursery school to university, establishing Our Saviour Girls Secondary School in Aba in 1990 and OSISATECH Girls Secondary School in Enugu in 1992. This effort is strategically geared towards closing the gap between girl child and boy child education and working to accomplish MDGs Number 3.

Automatic Employment on Graduation: As the saying goes, an idle man is the devil's workshop. In the current global economic crisis, it is common sense that education without employment is a recipe for humiliation and social vice. As a way of integrating male and female graduates into the labor market, Edeh often gives them automatic employment in his various outfits. This way, they become assets to the nation early in life. The MDGs should also include policies and programs that could enhance the creation of jobs for graduates to avoid unemployment related social hazards.

Special Weekly Orientation for Students: Greatness starts in the mind and success is determined by the values we appropriate. While some people are motivated from within, others are more inspired from without and Edeh understands the power of inspiration as a key to his own success. For this reason, he has made it mandatory in all his tertiary institutions for students to attend a 3 hour weekly orientation session for such inspiration.

At Madonna University in Elele, which has a massive number of students, every Monday morning from 6:00 to 9:00 a.m. is specially dedicated to the orientation program for female students (their male counterparts have their session on Tuesdays). Caritas University students in Enugu have the same session on Thursday from 7:00 to 10:00 a.m. One of the merits of this program is that it inspires students to develop self- confidence in order to better their lives and society.

Female students are encouraged to work hard to overcome gender barriers and to see men as their intellectual equals. Through this program, Edeh empowers his students, both male and female, psychologically and intellectually, giving them the necessary mind-set to propel them to success. The United Nations, through UNESCO, should consider introducing such a program to public schools to enhance the achievement of MDGs Number 3.

2.4.6: Edeh: Paragon of Environmental Sustainability

Edeh's environmental sustainability apparatus is built on the following principles:

- The concept of humans as "good that is"
- Sound environmental education in his institutions
- His charitable works across the globe for the survival of humans who are the principal occupants of the environment
- Madonna International Charity Peace Award (MICPA)
- Other operational tools, including EPTAism

Nature has necessitated that we rely on our immediate surroundings for food and shelter and our surroundings contain much of what we need. Unfortunately, our environment is being depleted because of our self-centeredness, as we have colonized, dominated, and conquered rather than appreciated and ennobled nature from which we may derive freedom, harmony, and peace.

Regrettably, we no longer act for the common good as we did in the days when communalism was the heartbeat of social cohesion. The human environment is continuously dilapidating due to egoistic government policies, *unmoderated* technological advancement, armed conflict, socioeconomic crisis and of course natural disaster. Often, our environment suffers because of our self-imposed ecological tragedy.

The Biotic and Abiotic Components of the Environment

The word *environment*, although we use it every day, is a complex term. Because of our diverse culture, belief, tradition, education, and philosophies of life, we define the word differently and various schools of thought have provided their own simplified definitions. Some define *environment* as the natural place where people, animals and plants live. Others define it as the external factors, such as light or the sources of energy, influencing the life of organisms. It can also be defined as the conditions surrounding people and affecting the way they live.

However, this word environment, with its stem *environ*, meaning "surroundings," is perhaps more understandably defined simply as the surroundings in which people live. In these surroundings are everything, both living and nonliving things of all varieties. In strict scientific terms, these living and nonliving things are called *biotic* and *abiotic*, respectively. The basic constituents of the environment are water, air, land, plants, and animals, with the non living components, water, air, and land, making up the abiotic components and the living components, the animals, plants, and microorganisms, constituting the biotic components.

The natural environment consists of all the living and nonliving things occurring naturally on earth. This environment is essentially self-supporting and requires minimal human management for maintenance, without any necessary active or economic inputs from man for its sustenance. It is therefore a complete ecological unity without massive human intervention. The natural environment can be broken down into physical and climatic components. The physical components are those things we can see, touch, and feel, such as hills, mountains, valleys, plains, rivers, lake, seas, coastline, animals and plants. In contrast, climatic components are things we can sometimes see and feel but cannot always touch, such as radiation, sunshine, wind, pressure, humidity, precipitation, and clouds.

Organisms constantly interact with their environment and this interaction is necessary for the transfer of energy from one component, biotic or abiotic, to another. *Ecosystem* is the term generally used to describe this interaction, collaboration, and cooperation of organisms for which by aggregating together, form a community and influence the lives of other organisms.

All those ways humans maltreat the environment have created an ecological calamity. Human activities have led to the destruction of biodiversity, jeopardizing the richness of species and genetic variability. Our environmental impact started long ago, when humans discovered fire and extracted materials from the soil to produce tools for building, cultivating crops and other activities. In the constant quest to improve their living conditions, humans then devised means of making life more comfortable and convenient by exploiting the natural environment. Later, the Industrial Revolution made a great impact on humanity with the advent of so many different new activities and technologies, automobiles and chemicals in particular, that have taken their toll on the environment.

Today, the world is filled with so many technological products, including aircraft, ships, skyscrapers, luxurious automobiles and telecommunication devices and sophisticated technologies are now available to industries, including food, textile, chemical manufacturing; agriculture; health care; mining and war, all of which require resources from the environment. However, the environment is vital for our survival and all ecological and evolutionary changes are centered in nature.

Environmental Manipulation by Humans

Our capacity to manipulate our environment has its merits and demerits. The felling of trees is advantageous for construction, but it also leads to drought. With advancements in technology, our environment has become a source of materials for our comfort rather than a wilderness in which we hunted wild animals and sometimes faced threats to our survival. We are now able to communicate with people across states, countries and continents and machines have made life easier by saving us labor that strains the body. Our industrialization has greatly improved our well-being thanks to environmental manipulation by man.

However, industrialization has led to environmental destruction on a scale never seen in history and humans are systematically wreaking more havoc on the earth and further diminishing its natural resources. In nearly every region, the air is being befouled, the waterways polluted, the soils washed away, the land desiccated and the wildlife killed. Even the depths of the sea are not immune to pollution. Over time, the carbon and nitrogen cycles upon which all living things, including humans, depend for the maintenance and renewal of life have been irreversibly damaged.

Basically, industry and technology have generated other ecological imbalances as well. We generate radioactive waste, long-living pesticides and thousands of toxic and potentially toxic chemicals and put them into our food, water and air. The industries that create them also impact the environment. As cities expand into vast, densely populated urban belts, they further deplete raw materials. At this juncture, we seem to have forgotten that nature is what it is because of a balance between living and nonliving things.

Anything strong and powerful only exerts more and more power if left unchecked and our power over the environment will only expand, leading to more destruction if it is not controlled, worsening the din of noise pollution; the stresses created by congestion; the immense accumulation of garbage, sewage, and industrial waste; and the profligate destruction of precious raw materials. These by-products of industrialization also change natural ecosystem.

For how long shall we continue to compose our requiem? We have done more damage to the planet in a single generation than humans did for thousands of years. Unfortunately, humans continue to destroy nature and destabilize the ecosystem. In this manner, it is out of equilibrium. If the pace of destruction continues, it is terrifying to speculate about what lies ahead for the next generation. This menace may damage the very integrity of life for centuries.

The ecological crisis of the contemporary Age is worse than man has witnessed at any time in the past and we continue to lose biodiversity. It is therefore critical to emphasize that humanity depends upon the complexity of life and that his well-being and survival depend upon the long evolution of organisms into increasingly complex and interdependent forms.

Nature and Mma-di

Homo sapiens is the most developed living specie, and our intellect has given us dominance over the earth and we have trampled on all of it. We have refused to understand that the environment is an intrinsic part of our existence, as without the environment, we may not have existed at all or we could have probably remained as spirit only.

Edeh's Metaphysics considers the environment as part of *ife di* (being) and he underlines that all beings are good by virtue of their creation by God, the Supreme Good. Anthropologists Jolly and Plog are on the same page as Edeh, as they state: "Human beings are not separate from nature, or even in nature. Rather, we are of nature, one among its millions of species" (1979, 3).

Mma-di, the human being, depends on nature: "One of the most important manifestations of our position in nature is our dependence on the rest of nature. We, along with every other form of life, are part of a single ecosystem—a cycle of matter and energy that includes all living things and links them to the nonliving" (Jolly and Plog 1979, 4). In acknowledging the environment's relevance to human nature, Edeh adds to this: "Man is caught up within the boundaries of these two worlds. '*Uwa*' (the visible world) is evident since it is experienced by senses, especially those of sight and touch. 'Ani muo' (the invisible world) is to the Igbo a reality because it is an accepted fact of everyday activity" (1985, 74).

The Existence of Two Worlds in Edeh

The environment should be treated with care and reverence, according to Edeh's philosophy, for as he expounds on the existence of two worlds in Igbo metaphysics, he reminds us that "for the Igbos, that enveloping world is the abode of nonhuman spirits, both good and bad. Some of the good spirits or gods are the earth, sun, sea, sky and wind gods, as well as the gods of the chief crops" (1985, 76). Because the Igbos venerate the earth, sun, sea, wind, and sky (the environment), along with the gods of the chief crops (gods of fertility and nutrition), then there is no question for them about maintaining environmental health. In *Servant-Leader: Emmanuel M.P. Edeh, an Inspiration in Youth Empowerment and Poverty Alleviation*, Onyewuenyi (2011b) relates that Edeh's conceptual framework, like the African way of life, is neither atomistic nor analytic but is being holistic and synthetic, concerned with totality, comprehensiveness.

This is because Edeh's philosophy sees reality as an interdependence of the material, humans, environment and the invisible. In other words, reality is rooted in harmonious reciprocity and complementarity between the material and the immaterial. For Edeh puts it this way: "for all beings in the material universe, existence is a dual inter-related phenomenon" (1985, 77).

With this in mind, Africa should develop a policy that "serves the long-term interests of both the environment and economy" (William 1990, 17). In view of the idea of the harmony between the environment and the unseen, Edeh remarks:

> For the Igbos there is a functional unity of the physical, utilitarian world with the deified, unchanging world that has shed its materiality. This is the environment in which the Igbo people, like all other African peoples, are

born, live, and die. Immersed in this environment, the people naturally develop the conviction of the existence of two worlds. Because they are much more inclined to be practical than speculative, they tend to make the two worlds equally real, as if both were material. Thus, they express the spiritual concepts connected with the invisible world in a material mode (Edeh 1985, 77).

Odoemene (2009) also reminds us that every person and creature is directly or indirectly in relationship with every other person or thing as beings who share the same ecosystem and therefore we need to maintain the environment and work in harmony. He further notes that what the world needs most today are reconciliation, justice, and peace and as we know, these are the pillars of EPTAism and ECPM. In this light, we see that Fr. Edeh has devoted his life working on environmental sustainability along with other MDGs.

Because of his African philosophy that pairs words with action, Edeh has made practical contributions to environmental sustainability. In one effort, the Faculty of Environmental Studies at Caritas University in Enugu facilitates ecological enlightenment and crusade against environmental degradation and their students, too, are champions of environmental sustainability.

In this regard, Edeh is a servant-leader with the potential to heal himself and others. Onyewuenyi (2011b) comments that a leader such as Edeh is responsible for the development of a healthy environment that enables teaching and studying to promote the practice and learning of civic virtues. Through this avenue, Edeh the servant-leader shows the light on personal, corporate, institutional and public health.

Because of EPTAism, the Madonna International Charity Peace Award (MICPA) founded by Fr. Edeh has come to be and in an uninterrupted mission of practical and effective charity, the MICPA has traversed the continents of the world on efforts to assist victims of ecological disasters, including the victims of the 2010 earthquake in Haiti, the 2011 tsunami in Cambodia and the 2012 flood in Calabar, Nigeria. MICPA is usually accompanied with cash prize as a way of encouraging and continuing the works of charity in different circumstances and the beneficiaries have so far received the award (MICPA) worth thousands of dollars.

MDGs Assessment: Ensuring Environmental Sustainability

Target: Integrate the principles of sustainable development into policies and programs and reverse the loss of environmental resources.

Progress Report

The *MDGs Report 2012* recorded achievement on environmental sustainability but it is observed that a lot still needs to be done. Asia has seen a reduction in forest loss, but the whole world has not reversed the loss. Forests present many advantages, including improvements in the environment as a whole and wildlife. There are economic benefits from tourism and this has led some governments to initiate campaigns for citizens and residents to plant trees.

More of the earth's surface is being protected all the time, even though biodiversity continues to be lost. The MDG target for drinking water has been realized ahead of schedule, although sub-Saharan Africa is still behind. Moreover, the percentage of urban slum dwellers in developing countries has reduced, although the absolute percentage is still high (UN MDGs Report, 2012).

The environment is essential to human life therefore humans should keep the environment safe for habitation. A healthy environment elongates human life, just as a polluted environment poses a danger to human life. Environmental degradation is sometimes caused by natural disasters, but humans are a principal architect of this menace. It is therefore necessary that every person must be conscious of how his or her actions affect the environment and efforts should be made to keep the environment healthy for human existence, complementing the MDG target with individual and private organizational efforts. The environment is our common home, and deserves to be healthy, for a healthy environment leads to human security.

> In essence, human security means safety for people from both violent and non-violent thrusts. It is a condition of being characterized by freedom from pervasive threat to people's rights, their safety or even their lives. It is an alternative way of seeing the world, taking people as its

point of reference, rather than focusing exclusively on the security of territory or governments. Like other security concepts—national security, food security (Don Huber, as cited in Ogaba 2004, 76–77).

The sanity of the environment is without question important in this way, since humans are at the center of the environment. Furthermore, human development cannot be realized if humans are not secured because of environmental conditions. Development, as Waterston (1976) defines it, is a multifaceted process that involves changes in structure and attitudes. It also embraces changes in institutions and the acceleration of economic growth, reduction in inequality and eradication of hunger and poverty. There is an undeniable connection between development, human security, and the environment.

The major challenges to environmental sustainability, according to the *MDGs Reports 2012*, are the lack of protection for most species, unequal progress between rural areas and urban areas in accessibility to water. In particular, poor sub-Saharan people lack access to clean drinking water more than rich sub-Saharan people, and access to sanitation also varies according to wealth and residence in sub-Sahara Africa too and the target for sanitation is still far from being realized, irrespective of the other improvements in developing regions (UN MDGs Report, 2012) In view of this, it is a global scandal that so many people are still subject to the health hazards associated with lack of sanitation and wealth.

It is unbelievable that in this day and age, people still cannot access clean drinking water. Unfortunately, the incidence of waterborne diseases is still high in Africa. It is common sense that good drinking water is the most fundamental human need, for humans cannot live without clean water.

The disparity in sanitation between the rich and the poor is alarming and for the poor to lack access to sanitation is tantamount to a terrible discrimination.

Sustainable development requires that we take a holistic approach to environmental issues, for it is certain that if environmental resources are allowed to be further depleted because of reckless use, humans will suffer both in the short term and in the long term. Our ecosystem must be protected and treated with care if we are to avert man-made and natural disasters.

It is a good a thing, then, that the United Nations has aroused global consciousness about sustainable development. This type of development does not happen by accident as it is usually willed, planned, and sacrificed for. The Brundtland Commission, a world commission on the environment, explains in its 1987 report that sustainable development is development to meet human needs now with consideration for the possibility of future generations to meet their needs as well (WCED 1987).

To achieve sustainable development, the world must reverse global warming, the increase in world temperature otherwise called climate change, for it causes sea levels to rise and has the potential to increase the intensity of extreme weather events and change patterns of precipitation. The aims of sustainable development may be fantasies if the world does not reverse global warming. Also, "settlement planning is central to ensuring that urban development and management meet sustainable development goals" (UNCHS 1996, 259).

Perennial Environmental Consciousness: Having seen Edeh's notion of the environment with the environment being a creation of Chineke and therefore good, we know that the environment is part of the Philosophy of *mma-di* and deserves care and protection. This philosophy leads to perennial environmental consciousness in EPTAism. To achieve MDG 7, the United Nations should start an awareness campaign to deliver this philosophy to all nooks and crannies of the world, just as Edeh does through his religious ministry, academic institutions and other outlets.

Provision of Sanitary Facilities: As we noted earlier, one of the challenges noted in the *MDGs Report 2012* is the continual lack of access to sanitation, which poses many health hazards to people around the globe. It is unfortunate that people must still defecate outdoors. The United Nations should collaborate with the governments of the world to formulate policies making it mandatory for organizations and institutions of service to the public to provide toilets for their staff members and visitors. Edeh's institutions all have such facilities.

Accessibility to Clean Drinking Water: According to the *MDGs Report 2012* some people in sub-Saharan Africa still lack access to clean drinking water irrespective of the fact that water is necessary for human life. In order to overcome this, Edeh's ministry produces Pilgrim Water, which is certified as good for drinking and available in all his institutions.

Provision of Staff Accommodations: No individual can afford to provide accommodation to the whole world, though shelter is a basic human need. Edeh provides accommodation to a good number of his employees and their families for their comfort and security. The United Nations should encourage other institutions to offer similar accommodations in order to facilitate MDGs Number 7.

Environmental Studies: Since the environment is fundamental to human existence, Edeh has made the study of the environment an integral academic program at his tertiary institutions. These programs inform the public about environmental issues, thus contributing to the checking of environmental hazards. Caritas University in Enugu has a faculty of environmental studies which also serves as a crusader of environmental cleanliness. In this vein, the UN should encourage the adoption of environmental education in universities for easier actualization of MDGs Number 7.

2.4.7: Edeh: Champion of Global Partnerships for Development

The collaboration of world countries, especially developed countries with developing countries, is a key MDG. With the level of economic disparity between developed and developing countries, it is certain that more than mere political rhetoric is required to achieve this goal.

Humans have devised means of understanding, dominating, and conquering nature and the universe. We have explored almost every part of our planet and have turned our focus to outer space. The world has witnessed continuous progress in science and technology to solve human problems and improve living condition of people around the world. The present day is distinct from previous era because of our focus on science and technology and today, science and technology provide hope for the future of humanity.

Despite this hope, however, science and technology also provide us with anxiety. Wars around the world in the modern Age have been fought with weapons made fierce by science and technology and some countries today are engaged in a constant show of strength through nuclear armaments and other weapons of mass destruction.

Countries of the world have seen many benefits from the good scientific and technological achievements. Mechanization in agriculture has come to stay and factories can mass produce goods and services. Because of science and technology, the world has witnessed a revolution in mass media and telecommunications.

The question that still puzzles a rational mind, then, is why the world is still divided between rich and poor despite these advancements. Why are some people still dying of hunger while others have plenty? In short, can the MDGs actually succeed in the development of international partnerships which could reasonably close the gap between the rich and poor nations? Only time will tell.

Edeh's Philosophy of Mma-di: The Key to International Partnerships

Edeh has strategically built mechanisms for global partnership development.

He has established a chain of international partnerships for human development in line with his idiosyncrasies. While countries of the world often wait to develop partnerships because of bureaucratic inefficiency, financial assistance from international financial institutions and other forms of aid from richer countries, Edeh's personal measures do not suffer from such delays. Everyone knows how difficult it is to service international debts, not to mention to fully repay them. Must people stand with their arms folded as they wait for international cooperation in this manner?

For the advancement of international growth and relationships, which are the fundamental aims of MDGs Number 8: Development of Global Partnership for Development, Edeh strategically embarks on practical, humanitarian, religious and empowerment initiatives. At the center of this exercise is his philosophy of *mma-di*, which puts into consideration the oneness of man in the world irrespective of his geographical location.

Edeh's human capital development initiatives, transnational charity, religious foundation, academic institutions, multidimensional empowerment schemes, and Justice, Reconciliation, and Peace Center could not have come to be if he had not conceived of humans as *mma-di*. Through his Mission of Practical and Effective Charity in symmetry with EPTAism, these efforts have led to extensive human development in different parts of the world, thereby strengthening international partnerships.

MICPA: A Medium for International Development and World Peace

The Madonna International Charity Peace Award (MICPA) recognizes those who not only do charitable works but also promote charity in any part of the world, and, as Ezechi Chukwu (2013) remarks, it is geared towards global partnerships for development.

Through MICPA, Fr. Edeh provides financial support across nations and continents as he honors those distinguished agents of charity. The MICPA, which is an annual event usually holds in the month of November at Madonna University Elele. MICPA contributes in no small way to international development, as it has benefitted victims of earthquakes, motherless babies' homes, victims of tsunami, victims of flood, and many more people.

Edeh's Approach to Employment: Aimed at International Cooperation, Development and World Peace

Edeh the thinker and philosopher contributes strategically to the building of global partnerships for development through his approach to employment, which cuts across countries and continents. Edeh, through African philosophy, is committed to giving gainful employment to people across the globe and these efforts institutionalize oneness in the global family and enhance practical developmental partnerships among nations. On his payroll are nationals of Nigeria, Cameroon, the Philippines, Germany and more countries, reflecting Fr. Edeh's peculiar commitment to international cooperation and world peace.

With the coming together of all these employees from different parts of the globe, Edeh has succeeded in making his institutions in general a community of *mma-di* in which cultures converge, interact and develop together with the aim of achieving peace. This is possible because the heartbeat of these relationships is love and care for others.

Hossein Daneschumand, a physician from Germany who specializes in obstetrics and gynecology, has been on the medical team at Madonna University Teaching Hospital for some years. He says of his employment: "I came to Madonna University Teaching Hospital through the instrumentality of Rev. Fr. Prof. Edeh. He visited my hospital in Germany and in the course of our interaction I discovered there was agreement of interest, what I mean here is the interest to care for others" (The Saviourites Magazine 2012/2013, 28). Daneschumand's testimony shows Edeh's desire to care for others and to build bridges across nations.

Education in Edeh: Key to Global Partnership Development

Edeh insists that his students carry the values of peace and love into the world with them after graduation, so Edeh the teacher imparts EPTAism to his students. Thousands of those students of his tertiary educational institutions are now gainfully employed around the world, preaching and practicing the precepts of EPTAism learned from Fr. Founder.

National Pilgrimage Center/National Shrine: A Religious Dimension to Global Partnership for Development

Another important dimension to Global Partnership for Development within the Edehist context is the Pilgrimage Center of Eucharistic Adoration and Special Marian Devotion in Elele, which was elevated to the status of a National Pilgrimage Center; a National Shrine on November 30, 2012, making it the first of its kind in Africa. The ceremony was presided over by the Papal Nuncio in Nigeria, His Excellency the Most Rev. Augustine Kasujja, who led the celebration of the solemn Eucharist.

This pilgrimage center attracts the faithful from all over Africa and many other parts of the world, who go there to pray and return to give testimonies of how their prayers have been answered. When one asks God for prosperity and God answers that prayer, the success extends to the society in which that person lives. So, all those pilgrims from around the world return home empowered, revived, and rebuilt. Thus, they are better, able to improve their lives and contribute to the development of their countries and to society in general.

Furthermore, what a thing stands for determines why it is sought after. Edeh stands for care, love, and peace and the ideals of charity, reconciliation, justice, and peace which are preached at the pilgrimage center. Certainly, these are the virtues which the people who flock there pray to achieve. Thus, adding to Edeh's practical contributions to the development of global partnership. Humans are spiritual and moral beings and to undermine this essential nature is to misconstrue them for objects. By adding a religious dimension to global partnership for development, Edeh integrates an important ingredient to his pro MDGs related agenda.

MDGs Assessment: Development of Global Partnership for Development

Target: Address the special needs of the least developed countries, landlocked countries, and small island developing states

Progress Report

The realization of MDG Number 8: Development of Global Partnership for Development is fundamental to the realization of all the other MDGs, for they all require the collaboration of UN member nations, especially the help of the developed nations. The *MDGs Report 2012* notes increased access to the international market for developing countries because of a reduction in barriers to those markets by developed countries. The report also notes that the least developed countries now benefit from preferential treatment from richer countries. Also, developing countries now boast of a rise in cell phone subscriptions and a downward trend in developing countries' debt (UN MDGs Report, 2012).

The world today is a global community and thanks to modern technology, especially in communication and transportation, countries' borders are more open and countries of the world become more interdependent and work in collaboration, having realized that no nation can survive in isolation no matter how rich it is. Richer countries should understand that they need the developing countries' economies as avenues for investment and new markets for their products. Placing stringent barriers on developing countries will not benefit developed nations much. Therefore, it is commendable that such constraints have been reduced, according to the *MDGs Report 2012*.

In the paper "Renewing the Commonwealth for the 21st Century: Policy Perspectives," Oduntan and Akinrinade (2004) ascribe to international organizations the need to work towards the development of their member nations, as the need for development is the major problem confronting many nations and Africa in particular, hence the establishment of the New Partnership for Africa's Development (NEPAD).

To accomplish MDGs Number 8, other existing international agencies such as FAO, UNESCO, UNICEF, IMF, WTO, WHO, IBRD, ILO, and WFP should give consistent support to nations and cooperate with one another to fast-track the achievement of the other MDGs and they should ensure that their programs are not opposed to the aims and achievements of the MDGs.

For the sake of clarity, Article 1(3) of the United Nations Charter (1945) states that the purpose of the UN, among other things, is the achievement of international cooperation in solving international problems of an economic, social, cultural, and humanitarian nature. Furthermore, the UN seeks to promote respect for human rights and to seek fundamental freedoms for all peoples of the world without distinction by sex, race, language, or religion. The world today is under the canopy of the UN and because of that, all its agencies should complement one another to promote peace and security throughout the world.

Decline in average tariffs have been recorded only for agricultural products in 2010, in the realm of exports from developing countries and the least developed countries, according to the *MDGs Report 2012*. While a good percentage of Internet users are now in developing countries, rates of use are behind in Africa, especially in sub-Saharan Africa. The decline of debt burdens in some regions is evident, although a decline in export earnings continues.

International monetary policy should be restructured to integrate the developing countries into the global market in a more meaningful way. The fact that average tariffs have declined for agricultural products only poses a great challenge. The problem of debt is also a major constraint to development and the conditions attached to such debts sometimes render the debt counterproductive. Sub-Saharan Africa is continuously behind according to many accepted international indices. It is therefore important that international policies be formulated to carry sub-Saharan Africa along in ongoing global development efforts.

With honest commitment, collaboration and dedication, the MDGs could bring about a worthwhile paradigm shift to the world, but efforts to accomplish the entire package must go beyond words. To accomplish MDGs Number 8 which is the creation of a partnership for international development, developed countries must make some sacrifices and participate with goodwill, as "simply providing more aid and debt relief without changing the rules of the game is not a solution to global poverty. Justice and sustainability are better long-term solutions than benevolence" (Ugorji 2009, 71).

Industrialized nations should also reshape international trade in order to meaningfully accommodate the developing nations and they must act in genuine solidarity, recognizing that the best way to provide aid is to guide the latter towards self reliance rather than perpetual dependence. This is certain because to be the principal agent of one's own development is a route to sustainable growth. The developing countries therefore, need to be empowered in the process of achieving the partnership for global development, for if they are perennial receivers only, the partnership will be lopsided.

Humanity as the Focus of Development

Edeh's philosophy places humans squarely at the center of development. The global developmental divide between north and south exists partly because the world is yet to adopt the Edehist notion of human as "good that is" and these unnecessary barriers that humans have created for selfish political reasons only further fan the embers of developmental imbalance and economic disparity between countries of the world. The world must accept that "good that is" is the same all over the globe.

It is quite difficult for the world to achieve a full-fledged global partnership for development unless humanity's ontological status is acknowledged. Edeh is of the conviction that the moment humans are genuinely accepted as *mma-di* by the international community, all efforts toward the achievement of international partnership and development will be successful. This is what Edeh believes in, stands for and has practiced for close to three decades, achieving practical results.

Creation of Jobs: Better than Aid and Loans from International Financial Institutions

While some thinkers, politicians, consultants, and economists think that aid from international financial institutions to developing countries is the ultimate solution, Edeh believes instead that the creation of jobs for all categories of workers is a sustainable antidote to underdevelopment and economic gaps between nations, for debts usually weigh down the pace of development in the indebted countries.

The situation is worse if the borrowing government is corrupt, which is common. Such countries consequently suffer and servicing or repaying the loan becomes impossible. This is why Edeh, in the application of his philosophy that harmonizes thought and action, prefers to create jobs. Edeh has carried out this task for almost three decades and the results are amazing. The UN should consider re-strategizing its policies for accomplishing the MDGs, by embracing job creation for development as an alternative to governments procuring loans from the likes of Paris Club because of the devastating consequences of such loans, especially when they could not be serviced or paid.

Review of Internet Liberalization

The UN has recorded overwhelming achievements in telecommunications in general and in global access to the Internet in particular. However, these achievements should be furthered with care. The world should not be distracted by the proliferation of modern communication to the extent that it ignores technology's inherent drawbacks. A situation in which youths have uncontrolled access to obscene materials on the Internet is alarming. This is not the type of advancement an international partnership for development should aim at.

Therefore, efforts should be made to control access to materials on the Internet with a focus on morality, for we should also talk of spiritual and moral developments, not just material developments alone. This is another component of EPTAism that the UN should consider for the sake of a better world and genuine development across the board.

The Peculiarity of the MICPA

The MICPA is a powerful tool that Edeh uses to complete his mission of practical and effective charity internationally. The MICPA is a special effort because of the special recognition it provides along with practical support for those who are at the forefront of charity anywhere in the world. To accomplish the MDGs, the UN should try to design a similar framework like the MICPA, so as to assist those who are genuinely involved with charity.

Funding fake NGOs and other bastardized political organizations operating under the guise of humanitarian groups does not achieve development. The activities of these groups need to be periodically assessed in order to ascertain the legitimacy and efficacy of their work, before they could receive funding from UN-related donor agencies. Through the MICPA, Edeh targets those who are involved with genuine practical activities to this end.

Through the MICPA, Edeh humbly adds value to a global partnership for development and shows that such a partnership does not have to be concerned only with the signing of agreements. Development is meaningful only when it achieves human growth by considering the ontological nature of humans irrespective of location. This is what Edeh champions through awarding the MICPA without considering religion, ethnicity, country, academic qualification, profession, or skin color. The advancement of the welfare of *mma-di* anywhere through genuine charity is the focus of the MICPA.

Religion as an Agent of International Development

Finally, Edeh adds to the international partnership for development from a religious dimension because he regards humans as spiritual beings, and their development must also be considered from a spiritual dimension. Through the National Pilgrimage Center, he enhances the spiritual and moral lives of people from around the world. Hence, reverend fathers, reverend sisters, reverend brothers, nuns, monks and other religious leaders work in his religious foundations throughout the world to spiritually form people and perpetuate EPTAism and Edeh's mission of practical and effective charity.

General Conclusion

The path to human development naturally goes uphill, for humans are at the center of creation. It is certain that no matter how much we try to deny our freewill, we demonstrably exercise it and we are responsible for our actions. Therefore, we cannot pretend that we have no hand in the problems of racism, underdevelopment, and disunity that are rampant around the globe. We cannot wash our hands off the injustices we see in different areas of human life.

Global oneness and growth can be achieved, as we can use our intellect to understand and willingly do the right thing for the common good of society. All people, institutions, organizations, governments and international bodies have roles and responsibilities to promote the human development. After all, the world is made up of human beings and the fundamental characteristic of humans is rationality.

To whom much is given, much is expected. The United Nations, being the highest governing body in the world therefore is expected to play important role in the management of human life. Its efforts, since its beginning are well known. However, the UN is often handicapped in the effective implementation of its policies and programs because of bureaucratic bottlenecks. It has proved to be toothless when world powers clash and often it lacks the wherewithal to accomplish concrete implementation of its programs.

The Millennium Development Goals, as we have seen, are a wonderful roadmap for the betterment of humanity and the Millennium Declaration that preceded the MDGs is also a very appealing working document. But it is one thing to have a good idea and another thing is to realize that idea in real life. The *MDGs Report 2012* affirms the success in achieving certain targets but the elusiveness of that success in achieving others. While the program should continue, it should be innovated with new ideas and effective strategies for a more rapid realization of the desired results. The strategy of Emmanuel Edeh, because of the overwhelming results it has yielded, should be incorporated into efforts to achieve the MDGs.

We have assessed Edeh's contributions towards achieving the MDGs and his efficacious *modus operandi* so that it may be strategically put forward to accomplish the MDGs. The viability of an idea and not who originated it is what matters. Edeh started his efforts toward human capital development, education, empowerment, religion and global development a decade and a half before the MDGs were set and his recorded successful results are evident. There is nothing wrong with the United Nations borrowing the model that has proved to be functional, responsive, pro-m*ma-di, mma-di* centered, and peace yielding over the decades.

At this point, the dimensions of Edeh's philosophy are worthy of consideration. His philosophy of a human being as "good that is" is an important step towards not only the realization of the MDGs but the attainment of peace. The MDGs are human-centered aims and that is why it is necessary to make efforts towards them with an understanding of human nature as Edeh considers it, as *mma-di*, as Edeh has persistently done.

Edeh has successfully contributed abundantly to all the eight MDGs. In addition, he has used other vital operational tools that the UN has not yet incorporated into the MDGs: the first is moral education, as offered in Edeh's institutions; the second is the distinctive motivational nature of the MICPA; and the third is religion, which is not given a voice in the MDGs. These keys, in addition to other efforts of Edeh, make up a strategic approach to development that has enabled Edeh to distinguish himself as the model of human empowerment without borders. Thus, thanks to Emmanuel Edeh, in this period of global economic, political, and religious crisis, when unity seems to be elusive, peace still seems achievable.

References

Abanuka, B. 1994. *A New Essay on African Philosophy*. Nsukka: Spiritan Publications.

Adigwe, Zulu. 2011. *A Biography of Very Rev. Prof. Emmanuel Edeh*. Enugu: Madonna University Press.

Agbo, Edmund Ugwu. 2012. In *Edeh's Charity Peace Model (ECPM)* First and Second Edition, Edited by Nicholas N. Chukwuemeka. Enugu: Madonna University Press.

Amah, Peter. O. 2012. *Inspiring 21st Century Africans to Serve-First*. Enugu: Madonna University Press.

Bourne, R. 2004. "Democracy, Human Rights and Commonwealth in the 21st Century: An Overview." *Nigerian Journal of International Affairs: The Future of the Commonwealth*. Volume 30, Number 2, 2004. pp. 11 – 21.

Buscaglia, L. 1978. *Personhood: The Art of Being Fully Human*. New Jersey: SLACK Incorporated.

Chibueze, O. G. 2009. "Improvisation and Utilization of Infrastructural Materials in Primary English Pedagogy: A Key to Achieving the Millennium Development Goals in Nigeria by 2015." *The Voice of Teachers*, Teachers Without Borders, Africa Regional Chapter, Abuja 1 (1).

Chukwu, Ezechi, ed. 2012. *Aspects of Edeh's Philosophy*. Vol. 2. Madonna University Press, Enugu.

———. 2013. "Edehization of the Millennium Development Goals." In *The Actualization of Millennium Development Goals: Fr. Edeh as a Pace Setter*. Enugu: Madonna University Press. Edited by Chukwu Ezechi.

Dabo, Lydia and Msheliza, Esther. 2009. "The Realization of the Millennium Development Goals (MDGs): The Association of Teachers Against

HIV/AIDS Model." *The Voice of Teachers,* Teachers Without Borders, Africa Regional Chapter, Abuja 1 (1).

Daniels, N. D. 1992. *Critical Issues: Protecting the African Environment.* New York: Council on Foreign Relations Press.

Ebo, C. 1989. "Formal Education: British and American Alternatives." In *Azikiwe and African Revolution,* edited by M. S. O. Olisa and Ikejiani-Clark. Ibadan: Africana-FEP Publishers.

Edeh, E. M. P. 1985. *Towards an Igbo Metaphysics.* Chicago: Loyola University Press.

————. 2006. *Peace toThe Modern World: A Way Forward Through the Concrete Living of the Existential Dictates of the African Philosophy of Being.* Banbury, UK: Minuteman Press.

————. 2009. *Igbo Metaphysics: The First Articulation of African Philosophy of Being.* Enugu: Madonna University Publications.

————. 2012. *Edeh's Charity Peace Model.* Enugu: Madonna University Press.

Egbekpalu, Purissima. 2011. "The Philosophical Anthropology of Edeh: An Existential Pathway to Global Peace." In *Aspects of Edeh's Philosophy,* vol. 2, edited by Ezechi Chukwu. Enugu: Madonna University Press.

Egbutah, E. U. 2009. "Food Security in Nigeria: Concept and Strategies for Improvement." *The Voice of Teachers,* Teachers Without Borders, Africa Regional Chapter, Abuja 1 (1).

Egonu, I. T. K. 2005. "The Concept of the Humanities." *African Humanities: Humanities and Nation Building.* Nsukka: Afro-Orbis Publications. Edited by Francis Anyika.

Ejiofor, P. 2004. In *Madonna University, a University with a Difference: A Brief History, Lectures and Addresses,* edited by E. M. P. Edeh. Enugu: Saviourite Publications.

Ellin, Joseph. 1995. *Morality and the Meaning of Life: An Introduction to Ethical Theory.* Orlando: Harcourt Brace College Publishers.

Eneh, Joseph. O. 2010. "Philosophy of Language and Hermeneutics in the Philosophy of Emmanuel Edeh." In *Madonna ISREPAT International*

Journal of African Philosophy and Theology, vol. 2, edited by Ugwu E. Agbo. Enugu, Madonna University Press.

Forrest, Diana. 1955. *The Adventurers: Ordinary People with Special Callings*. Winfield, British Columbia, Canada: Wood Lake Books.

Forrest, M. D. 1946. *The Fair Flower of Eden*. Saint Paul, MN: Radio Replies Press.

Garba, C. M. 2009. "Science Education and the Achievement of the Millennium Development Goals (MDGs) by 2015." *The Voice of Teachers*, Teachers Without Borders, Africa Regional Chapter, Abuja 1 (1).

Ifemesia, C. 1979. *Traditional Humane Living among the Igbo: An Historical Perspective*. Enugu: Fourth Dimension Publishing.

Jolly, C. J., and Plog. F. 1979. *Physical Anthropology and Archeology*. New York: Alfred A. Knopf.

Kanem, J. A. U. 2006. "Testimony by Prof. A. U. John Kanem." In *Peace to the Modern World: A Way Forward through the Concrete Living of the Existential Dictates of the African Philosophy of Being*. Banbury, UK: Minuteman Press.

Kayode, J. O. 1984. *Understanding African Traditional Religion*. Ile-Ife: University of Ife Press.

Kutai, M. A. 1999. *Challenges of Today's Youth: A Christian Perspective*. Jos: Owe Press.

Lazear, Jonathon. 1994. *Remembrance of Mother*. New York: Simon & Schuster.

Longshal, M. W., and M. Usman. 2009. "Achieving the Millennium Development Goals (MDGs) by 2015 through Effective Teaching of Agricultural Science in Nigeria." *The Voice of Teachers*, Teachers Without Borders, Africa Regional Chapter, Abuja 1 (1).

Maritain, Jacques. 1943. *Education at the Crossroads*. New Haven, Yale University Press.

———. 2005. *An Introduction to Philosophy*. London: Continuum.

Mfam, K. I. 2009. "Vocational and Technical Education: A Panacea for Achieving the Millennium Development Goals in Nigeria." *The Voice of Teachers*, Teachers Without Borders, Africa Regional Chapter, Abuja 1 (1).

Ngwoke, Bernard. 2006. "Testimony by Very Rev. Fr. Assoc. Prof. Bernard IK Ngwoke." In *Peace to the Modern World: A Way Forward through the Concrete Living of the Existential Dictates of the African Philosophy of Being*. Banbury: UK: Minuteman Press.

Nieuwenhuys, O. 2003. "Growing Up between Places of Work and Non-Places of Childhood."In *Children's Places: Cross-Cultural Perspectives*, edited by Karen Fog Olwig and Eva Gullov. New York: Routledge.

Nouwen, H. J. M. 1994. *With Burning Hearts: A Meditation on the Eucharistic Life*. Maryknoll, NY: Orbis Books.

Nwoye, Chukwugozie Donatus C. 2013. "The Contributions of Fr. Emmanuel Edeh to Poverty Eradication of Extreme Poverty and Hunger." In *The Actualization of Millennium Development Goals: Fr. Edeh as a Pace Setter*. Enugu: Madonna University Press.

Nze, C. B., ed. 2011. *Aspects of Edeh's Philosophy.*Vol. 1, Enugu: Madonna University Press.

Nzomiwu, J. P. C. 1985. In *The Igbo Church and Quest for God*, edited by Chukwudubem B. Okolo. Uruowulu-Obosi, Anambra: Pacific College Press.

Odoemene, A. N. 2009. "The Millennium Development Goals and the Church Service to Reconciliation, Justice and Peace in Africa." In *The Church of Jesus the Saviour in Africa*, vol. 1 (Lineamenta), organized and edited by E. M. P. Edeh. Enugu: Madonna University Press.

Oduntan, Tunde and Akinrinade, Sola . 2004. "Renewing the Commonwealth for the 21st Century: Policy Perspectives." *Nigerian Journal of International Affairs* 30 (2).

Ogaba, Uche. 2004. "The Commonwealth and the Imperatives of Conflict Management and Human Security in Africa." *Nigerian Journal of International Affairs* 30 (2).

Okafor, D. C. 1994. *Towards Integrated Nationhood*. Owerri.

Okwudili, Mike Ike. 2011. "Education from Edeh's Philosophy of Thought and Action (Eptaism)." In *Aspects of Edeh's Philosophy*, vol. 2, edited by Chukwu Ezechi. Enugu: Madonna University Press.

Oladipo, O. 2009. *Philosophy and Social Reconstruction in Africa*. Ibadan: Hope Publications.

Omeogo, M. G. 2009. "Jobs for the Jobless in the Life of Fr. Edeh." In *Authentic Human Development: Insights from The Metaphysics of Rev. Fr. Prof. Edeh*, edited by Onyema Uzoamaka. Enugu: Madonna University Press.

Onukwube, Lawrence C. 2012. "The Establishment of Caritas University in Enugu: Motivation and Expectation towards Peace." In *Man and Peace: In the Light of Edeh's Philosophy of Thought and Action (EPTAISM)*, edited by R. Onyewuenyi. Enugu: Madonna University Press.

Onyewuenyi, Remy. 2009. *The Mustard Seed of Jesus the Saviour in Elele*. Enugu: Madonna University Press.

———. 2010. *Emmanuel M. P. Edeh, Man of Peace and His Works*. Enugu: Madonna University Press.

———. 2011a. In *Aspects of Edeh's Philosophy*, vol. 2, edited by Ezechi Chukwu. Enugu: Madonna University Press.

———. 2011b. *Servant-Leader: Emmanuel M. P. Edeh, An Inspiration in Youth Empowerment and Poverty Alleviation: The Nigerian Experience*. Enugu: Madonna University Press.

Otonko, Jake Omang. 2009. "Africa and the Challenge of Integral (Integrated) Formation of Priests in (the Understanding of) the 21st Century Synod of Africa." In *The Church of Jesus the Saviour in Africa*, vol. 1 (Lineamenta), organized and edited by E. M. P. Edeh. Enugu: Madonna University Press.

Plato. 1969. *The Collected Dialogues of Plato*. Edited by Edith Hamilton and Huntington Cairns. Bollingen Series LXXI. New York: Pantheon.

Raz, J. 1975. *Practical Reason and Norms*. London: Hutchinson & Co.

Reisine, Susan T and Fifield, Judith. 1988. "Defining Disability for Women and the Problem of Unpaid Work." in *Psychology of Women Quarterly*.

Vol. 12, No. 4. Published by Cambridge University Press, for Thirty-five American Psychological Association.

The Saviourites Magazine 2012/2013. "Man in the Contemporary Society, A Challenge to Human Dignity." (1). Agbani.

Ross, R. 1983. *Prospering Woman: A Full Guide to Achieving the Full, Abundant Life*. Mill Valley, CA: Whatever Publishing.

Shaffer, J. A. 1968. *Philosophy of Mind*. New Jersey: Prentice-Hall.

Shagari, Shehu. 1982. "Education: The Greatest Investment for Development." In *The Challenge of Change: Collected Speeches of President Shehu Shagari*, vol. 3. Lagos: Federal Department of Information, Domestic Publicity Division.

Siegel, Bernie. 2004. "Understanding Why." In *Open My Eyes, Open My Soul: Celebrating Our Common Humanity*, created by Yolanda King and Elodia Tate. New York: McGraw-Hill.

Sofola, J. A. 1978. *African Culture and African Personality: What Makes an African Person African*. Ibadan: African Resources Publishers.

Ugorji, Lucius Iwejuru. 2009. "Restoring the Dignity of the Poor in Nigeria through the Millennium Development Goals." In *The Church of Jesus the Saviour in Africa*, vol. 1 (Lineamenta), organized and edited by E. M. P. Edeh. Enugu: Madonna University Press.

UN. 2012. *Millennium Development Goals Report 2012*. http://mdgs. un.org/unsd/mdg/Resources/Static/Products/Progress2012/ English2012.pdf.

———. 2013. "UN at a Glance." Accessed March 7, 2013 **http://www. un.org/en/aboutun/index.shtml**.

UN Centre for Human Settlements. 1996. *An Urbanizing World: Global Report on Human Settlements*. Oxford: Oxford University Press.

Unegbu, R. O. 2006. "Testimony by Prof. R. O. Unegbu." In *Peace to the Modern World: A Way Forward through the Concrete Living of the Existential Dictates of the African Philosophy of Being*. Banbury, UK: Minuteman Press.

UN General Assembly. 2000. Resolution 55/2. "United Nations Millennium Declaration." Accessed on March 8, 2013. http://www.un.org/millennium/declaration/ares552e.htm.

Uzoamaka, O., ed. 2009. *Authentic Human Development: Insights from the Metaphysics of Rev. Fr. Prof. Edeh*. Enugu: Madonna University Press.

Vredevelt, P. 1988. *Mothers & Sons: Raising Boys to Be Men*. Grand Rapids, MI: Fleming H. Revell.

Waterston, A. 1976. *Development Planning: Lessons of Experience*. Baltimore: John Hopkins Press.

William, K. R. 1990. "The Green Thumb of Capitalism: The Environmental Benefits of Sustainable Growth." *Policy Review* (Fall).

World Commission on Environment and Development. 1987. *The Brundtland Commission Report*. New York: The United Nations.

Wikipedia. 2013. "Millennium Development Goals." Accessed March 7, 2013

Article 1(3) of the United Nations Charter (1945)

http://en.wikipedia.org/wiki/Millennium_Development_Goals.

Oxford Advanced Learner's Dictionary

About the Author

Ezechi P.D. Chukwu, Ph.D is a Senior Lecturer and Chair of Philosophy Department, Caritas University Enugu Nigeria. He is a researcher and scholar with publications in local and international journals. Dr. Chukwu is happily married to his wife Ugochi and is blessed with four wonderful kids: Ugoeze, Chinenyeze, Obieze and Olaeze.

It is important to note that most of the ideas in this work were clearly given by Fr. Prof. Edeh whom we are discussing in this book.

www.ingramcontent.com/pod-product-compliance
Lightning Source LLC
Chambersburg PA
CBHW020540290526
45786CB00002B/967